BEHIND THE BLACK MASK

MY TIME AS AN ANTIFA ACTIVIST

GABRIEL NADALES

BOMBARDIER
B O O K S

BOMBARDIER BOOKS
An Imprint of Post Hill Press

Behind the Black Mask:
My Time as an Antifa Activist
© 2020 by Gabriel Nadales
All Rights Reserved

ISBN: 978-1-64293-732-9
ISBN (eBook): 978-1-64293-733-6

Cover art by Cody Corcoran
Interior design and composition, Greg Johnson, Textbook Perfect

Post Hill Press
New York • Nashville
posthillpress.com

Published in the United States of America

To my wife,
You are the best person I know.
Thank you for making me a better person.

CONTENTS

INTRODUCTION

AMERICA ON FIRE

On May 25, 2020, four Minneapolis police officers killed an African American man named George Floyd. A video of the incident, captured by a bystander, shows excessive force on the part of officer Derek Chauvin as he presses his knee into Floyd's neck for several minutes, even though Floyd was already in custody.

The viral images spread on social media like wildfire as conservatives, liberals, progressives, libertarians, and nonpolitical people alike denounced the officer's use of lethal force.

This tragedy should have been a unifying moment for Americans in which everyone could rally to reform police tactics. But instead of coming together, cities across the country burned at the hands of violent black-clad extremists—members of a shadowy group known as Antifa—who hijacked the justifiable indignation felt by numerous Americans, and used the anger as a springboard to push their radical left-wing agenda.

Antifa stands for antifascist, but the name is deceptive. For one thing, the very name is calibrated so that anyone who dares to criticize the group or its tactics can be labeled a fascist. Otherwise, why would someone oppose a group dedicated to fighting fascism? In turn, this allows Antifa members to justify violence against all who dare speak out against them.

The same goes for the Black Lives Matter (BLM) movement. Of course Black lives matter. But BLM uses the name and the slogan as a club to beat down anyone who criticizes its agenda or methods. In fact, Antifa's mission is not to fight fascism, and neither is BLM's mission to fight for black lives. Both movements are intent on pushing a left-wing revolutionary agenda while sugarcoating it with statements palatable to ordinary Americans.

Such a tactic is nothing new. Radical left-wing revolutionary politics often work this way. In fact, this political strategy has a name: it is known as the Mass Line.

The Mass Line was created by former Communist leader Mao Zedong, and it is the reason why China is a Communist country today. The purpose of the Mass Line is to "organize mass movements to create more favorable conditions for [a] socialist revolution."[1] Mass Line organizers infiltrate honest movements and inject them with Marxist ideologies while falsely claiming Communism to be the only solution to the struggle suffered by those within a particular group. Groups like Antifa and Black Lives Matter use important hot-button issues as a façade to divide Americans and push American society into a more favorable condition for a socialist revolution.

The protests in the wake of George Floyd's untimely death at the hands of Officer Chauvin are a natural part of America's grieving process. But the riots perpetrated by Antifa are a direct result of Mass Line organizing. Left-wing radicals hijacked the momentum felt by every American to push their extremist socialist agenda.

Yet many left-wing figures downplay the impact Antifa has had on the riots by claiming Antifa simply does not have the manpower to orchestrate such violence. Historian Mark Bray primarily made this claim in an interview on CNN when he stated that Antifa does not "get more than a couple hundred people" at each of its rallies.[2]

In part, Bray is correct. It would be dishonest to pretend that every single violent rioter was a member of Antifa. But it is more intellectually bankrupt to ignore Antifa's role in instigating the violence in key cities across the nation, and the George Floyd tragedy was the moment Antifa was waiting for to begin its uprising.

For example, an Antifa-affiliated group took to Twitter to ask for support in an operation against one of Minnesota's police precincts.[3] And in Portland, Oregon, Antifa activists chased and beat a man unconsciously merely because he was carrying an American flag.[4] And in Seattle, Washington, Antifa organizers occupied a police precinct, naming it the Capitol Hill Organized Protest (CHOP), or the Capitol Hill Autonomous Zone (CHAZ), and declared four blocks within the city autonomous from American soil.[5] Places like St. Paul, Minnesota; Portland, Oregon; Seattle, Washington; New York City; Austin, Texas; Chicago, Illinois; and Oakland, California, were some of the worst hit by left-wing violence because Antifa activists had been allowed to organize in these cities for several years prior. Antifa began the violence in these cities and set the narrative for the rest of the country's people to burn down their own communities.

While some continue to belittle Antifa's influence, others outwardly deny its existence, like Democratic Congressman Jerry Nadler, who called Antifa "imaginary."[6] Yet there is nothing imaginary about a black conservative journalist who was stabbed in the back by an Antifa terrorist.[7] And there is nothing imaginary about the three federal officers who were permanently blinded by Antifa through the use of lasers.[8] Antifa's existence is undeniable.

But Representative Nadler is not the only Antifa denier. In Seattle, Washington, as thousands of left-wing radical demonstrators established CHAZ, Seattle Mayor Jenny Durkan refused to condemn the Left's willful disregard for the rule of law for almost four weeks, calling the occupation a form of "patriotism."[9]

This Antifa-spearheaded project was an utter failure. During the day, the mainstream media portrayed the occupation as having the energy of a festival.[10] While at night, CHAZ was a place of violence in which a sixteen-year-old teen was murdered.[11] Many politicians refuse to see Antifa for the violent movement that it is because they blindly see the Antifa as an ally—since it opposes President Trump. Further, they fear that Antifa will target them next.

In many respects, Antifa and the radical Left have already claimed many victories. These leftist radicals have intimidated dozens of city councils across the nation into defunding their police departments, thereby neutering the police response to left-wing violence.

What happened to George Floyd is a tragedy, and Americans should work together so that such an incident is never repeated. But Antifa and the violent tactics that come with it are not the answer.

Yet I get the allure of Antifa—because I once belonged to it myself.

Like other Antifa activists, I remember being angry. Angry at police officers who I thought protected neo-Nazis. Indignant at Wall Street for stealing money from the poor. Aggravated at the mistreatment of animals in factory farms. Bitter at what appeared to be this country's endless foreign wars. Angry at corporations who polluted my neighborhood. Angry at a system I thought was stacked against me.

I first joined the radical antifascist movement because I believed it was the best vehicle to fight against the injustices in the American system of government. Only now am I mature enough to understand that Antifa is not fighting for justice or equality. The riots and occupation perpetrated by Antifa were a dishonor to the memory of George Floyd. They were not about demanding police reform to prevent future tragedies. The violence was targeted at destroying the private property of innocent Americans because Antifa hates capitalism and everything America stands for.

Sometimes mistakes are hard to admit. To do so places us in an uncomfortable position, where we are forced to confront our actions and our conscience. Even more challenging is to admit our errors to another. Becoming part of Antifa was the biggest mistake of my life.

The truth is that I expected this part of my life to be a mere footnote of my adolescence. I never expected to appear on Fox News and admit to the destruction of property. Nor did I plan to write an op-ed for The Hill, condemning my radical past. Yet at the time, I felt it necessary to break windows, spray graffiti, drop political banners off the side of buildings, and attend tumultuous rallies to fight against supposed fascists. At the time, I believed that if you do not fight for your values, you have none to stand on. Now, these narrow-minded actions seem like the mistakes of another person altogether.

I also never expected to be invited to universities throughout the country to speak to and advise conservative students. I planned to work for a policy think tank when I first majored in politics. Yet I have been a political activist for over ten years, and for the past seven, I have fought against institutionalized liberal bias throughout the country. My work has taken me to over thirty states, Puerto Rico, and D.C., to help conservative students fend off ideological discrimination.

To countless leftist students and administrators, being a conservative is equivalent to committing a heinous crime. Yet I am fortunate enough to speak to rooms filled with conservative and libertarian students who are eager to hear about my experiences as a radical leftist. As I tell them, I became an activist because I wanted to help people. But I became a conservative when I realized that many left-wing ideologies want to control people while merely appearing to help.

I always expected to keep my past a secret. Yet every day, I see cities around the country struggling to maintain peace amid the rise of left-wing political violence while liberal politicians deny Antifa's existence. I know I have a duty to speak up because if no one does, the Left will obliterate what it means to be a free American.

In fact, the George Floyd riots are merely the precursor for what Antifa and the radical Left have in store if President Trump wins re-election in November. If President Trump garners enough support on November 3rd, it is all too likely that the radical Left will denounce the election as illegitimate, and America will go through yet another period of unrest and violence perpetuated by Antifa-type activists.

This book is by no means a detailed study of Antifa or the anarchist tradition in general. What I write here comes from personal experience. The history I recount, and the motivations

I explore, come from countless conversations I engaged in with fellow anarchists while I was in the antifascist movement.

This book is also not a philosophical argument as to why Antifa is a thorn in America's side. These pages tell the story of a conservative activist whose job is to help protect conservative students from left-wing abuses.

Antifa is not solely responsible for all left-wing political violence. Not every attack by a left-wing radical is an Antifa attack. There are numerous left-wing militant organizations that are not part of the Antifa movement, such as the Weather Underground, which was active in America a decade before the first American Antifa group was organized. But Antifa exemplifies the worst of this dangerous ideology, which is becoming bolder and more prevalent in American society. Ever since President Donald J. Trump took office, the Left has sought any and every opportunity to intimidate, harass, and harm conservative and libertarian Americans.

This book explores left-wing political violence and intimidation, and the effects they have on American political discourse. Something, I am sad to say, I have experienced as both the perpetrator and a victim. I will recount numerous situations in which I have torn down police barriers, broken windows, and yelled threats at innocent people. But I will also convey the times I have been attacked by left-wing activists while I spread the conservative message on college campuses.

I decided to write this book for several reasons. First, I kept receiving requests to write one and tell my full story. The fifteen-to thirty-second sound bites I deliver on TV or at speaking events fail to paint what it was like to wear the black mask and march with Antifa. Second, I wanted to dispel some dangerous myths about Antifa. Unfortunately, mainstream news headlines over-simplify this radical movement. Antifa and anarchism are actually complex ideologies and ways of life, which I hope to explain. Lastly, I wanted to highlight the dangers of political violence—from all sides.

The history of radical activism that I know, I learned from a long line of activists before me. Some I befriended; others I only spoke to once or twice. Many were much more active than I was ever willing to be. Still, I was fortunate to meet many older anarchists and antifascist activists through several different venues. From talking to them, I learned a lot about the history of radical movements in America and Europe. Because anarchism is a counterrevolutionary movement, there are few authoritative books on the subject. Many document conflicting personal accounts. Therefore, the stories I heard were like a puzzle that I endeavored to assemble.

The puzzle took shape with every activist I spoke to. I learned about anarchism and Antifa by meeting these agitators at protests, rallies, meetings, and music performances. At anarchist book-fairs in Los Angeles and Orange County, I loaded my library with accounts of anarchist history. Not surprisingly, there was an abundance of anti-American propaganda at these events. The bookfairs also hosted workshops by "renowned" scholars who strove to "keep the anarchist tradition alive." Some venues and collectives published pamphlets or zines, which were available for free. I was also invited by friends to attend "historical tours" sponsored by the "Black Rose Historical Society," which kept the history of local anarchist and communist movements.

The tours themselves were just like any other historical tour I have ever attended, except they were led by left-wing anarchists and communists. Typically, they included about fifteen to twenty people from different cities around the county. Often, we met at an agreed-upon location and then visited up to twenty historical sites while our guide described the events that had occurred there a century earlier. The only sign of the group's political outlook is that two people carried an anarchist and a communist flag as we walked around the city. And at the end of the tours, we would all meet at a restaurant nearby to get to know one another.

At these tours, I always asked questions and learned history not taught in traditional history books. For example, I learned that the radical left-wing movement in America often finds commonalities with worker unions such as the International Workers of the World (IWW). In San Pedro, California, the IWW has a plaque dedicated to their movement, which I visited as part of an anarchist historical tour. With every conversation, meeting, or book I read, the puzzle became clearer. However, spoken tales often change with every retelling. Thus, my accounts of the history of radical activism may deviate from what other anarchists and extreme left-wing activists claim to have occurred. I witnessed this concept firsthand when I was part of the movement. While I was an anarchist, my friends and I routinely talked about the history of anarchism. We often spent hours debating the motivations of the previous generation of radical activists.

It's important to understand the main distinctions within the anarchist subculture. While I learned a lot of what I would call "hard-anarchist history," I was highly involved in the anarchist movement as an "anarcho-punk." There is a simple distinction between the two groups. First, a regular anarchist is mainly preoccupied with a stateless society and political activism. Their tactics may take many forms, while the activists often involve themselves with workers unions, collectives, or other national or subnational organizations that grow the radical left-wing movements. Meanwhile, anarcho-punks promote anarchist ideology and are engaged in the same type of direct action, but also submerge themselves in a subculture that uses popular music and style to spread the anarchist message. Since punk began, there have been many who are merely attracted to punk for its rebellious fashion. Anarcho-punks often call them "fashion punks," "chaos punks," or "drunk punks," in a derogatory manner. What's more, the contempt flows both ways. Many anarchists throw fits about anarcho-punks for caring too much about the subculture and not the anarchist movement, often referring to these types of activists as "lifestyle anarchists."

This criticism is an apt critique of many in the subcultural movement. Many punks like to go to shows to get drunk and fight while bands demand to be paid, and treat backyard gigs as if they were playing in Carnegie Hall. Many punks may pretend to be a counterculture to America, but they often establish a mirror image of the worst that society has to offer within their "movement."

However, I was an anarchist first and foremost. I became politically active not for the music, but for the message and ideology. I truly wanted to live free without the shackles of government. However, I was also a teenager. It was only natural that I was also attracted to the subculture, loud music, and rebellious lifestyle. While anarchists may find it easy to dismiss anarcho-punks as mere teenagers, many of them have done great things for the anarchist movement. In fact, modern Antifa was reborn in Great Britain and the United States through the punk-rock scene.

When I went to music shows, I met many subcultural figures who have had a significant impact on anarchist history. Some I was also able to speak with at length about their experiences as radical activists. One notable example was when I spoke with Steve Lake from the British band called Zounds. In the 1980s, he and other members of Crass Records were heavily politically involved. The Crass Collective made British national headlines when they were prosecuted for "obscene" publications for protesting British war policies.[12] I also met the vocalist of Resist and Exist, which is an anarcho-punk, animal rights band. His name is Jang Lee, but people call him Peace Punk, and he has been involved in the anarchist movement for decades in Southern California. He was one of the key organizers of the Southern California Anarchist Bookfairs. If they knew I would eventually become a conservative, I am sure they would not have given me the time of day back then. Or worse, they likely would have kicked me out of their events. Still, most of them enjoyed talking to the "younger generation of the resistance."

I would be in shock if they remembered me. But to be fair, I never gave them my real name. Speaking with all these figures, I learned more and more about the anarchist movement.

I understand why "serious" anarchists take issue with anarcho-punks like me. First off, we looked silly. Whenever I show pictures to my colleagues, they are shocked. These days, I work in D.C., and while I tend not to wear a tie, you may often find me wearing a suit to work. The only time I dress down is when I am on college campuses to advise conservative students.

Contrast that with sixteen-year-old me, who wore green, blue, or orange hair, typically spiked from six to nine inches with an immense amount of Elmer's glue. Yes, actual glue. The paste was one of the only materials able to support the length of the spikes, which were inspired by the Statue of Liberty. Other people also use gelatin or egg whites to achieve the same result. If you want to see what that would look like, just google "liberty spikes."

My clothing was equally provocative. My attire consisted of the same black jeans almost daily, which I sewed into skinny jeans, with dozens of band names stitched on. Whenever I actually changed pants, I wore a pair that I constructed from two existing pairs. One leg was black with patches, while the other was plaid. I often looked like a walking billboard advertising all these bands. I also wore brightly colored jackets, vests, combat boots, spikes, bondage belts, and bullet belt accessories. I may not have considered myself a fashion punk, but I certainly played the part.

In one incident, I boarded a bus on the Foothill Transit in the San Gabriel Valley of California. I wore half-black, half-green plaid pants and "charged" hair, which looks like Marv's hair when he was electrocuted in *Home Alone 2*. As I paid my fee, a woman in the back lost her self-control and broke out in laughter. As I walked past her toward the end of the bus, she peeked back to take another look while she failed to control her laughter. You could see me a mile away.

Yes, we looked silly. But the outlandish outfits also made it easier not to be recognized while wearing the simple black mask.

I spent a lot of time at music shows, aka gigs. I also spent countless hours recruiting more people from these places to get them to become more politically active. I wrote zines and pamphlets, and made merchandise to fund my activities. At the time, I found that all my efforts were worthwhile because I was able to organize with anarchists in Hollywood, the Inland Empire, and Los Angeles. I wanted to transcend the punk scene and bring back meaning to what it meant to be a rebel.

Yet I seldom spoke about my political activism with those who personally knew me. Sometimes I would mention vague platitudes about getting involved in the political system. Still, most people in school or outside of my activism merely saw me as "that punk kid." I was cautious to choose carefully whom I trusted and who could keep secret the things I did. When it comes to my parents, I am sad to say that I lied to them. I would often tell them I was doing a project or just going out with friends, when, in fact, I would spend all day at a protest or rally. No one I routinely hung out with was regularly politically active with me. Some of them may have attended a protest or two, but I would often find connections outside my immediate circle. I kept my personal life separate from my political activism. That is one of the many tactics I learned to practice. I never trusted anyone to know everything. I certainly never expected to tell a soul about my activism later in life. Even my wife was surprised when I first went on TV to talk about my antifascist past.

The first time I openly warned about Antifa's anti-American sentiment was in March 2017, in an op-ed for the *Washington Examiner*. I received some general questions from interested people, but did not reply to them. I was not interested in any publicity. I just wanted to say my piece and move on. I did not expect Antifa to become a prominent force in American politics. I certainly did not expect the movement to catch the attention of President Trump.

All of that changed in February 2018, when I saw my friend Hayden Williams brutally attacked at UC Berkeley, by Zachary Greenberg, without any provocation. Hayden was working as a field representative for the Leadership Institute, and I was his direct supervisor during the attack. As I remember it, Hayden and

I planned an activism event for the UC Berkeley chapter of Turning Point USA club, which I helped start. This event was only a couple days after Jussie Smollett was accused of staging his own hate crime in Chicago. To bring attention to the issue, Hayden created and held a sign that read, "Hate Crime Hoaxes Hurt Real Victims."

After tabling for some time, two men approached him and became belligerent. One of them began to yell obscenities at Hayden. In response, he pulled out his phone to record the interaction because he feared the situation would escalate. Then Zachary flanked him and began to beat Hayden numerous times. At first, Hayden struggled to get free, and he eventually did. However, Zachary persisted and landed a punch to Hayden's left eye, which rocked him back. Fortunately, Greenberg then walked away, albeit not before yelling antiwhite racist slurs at Hayden.

Hayden was fortunate that his altercation with Greenberg was filmed by a couple bystanders, providing two angles of the savage attack. Without that evidence, Hayden would have never met President Trump. He would never have spoken to a crowd of thousands at the Conservative Political Action Conference (CPAC), behind the presidential podium. More importantly, Zachary Greenberg would not be facing four felony charges in the state of California.

I have no reason to believe Zachary Greenberg is directly involved with Antifa-type groups. However, he does share their belief that it is OK to attack people over political disagreements. After that incident, I realized how hard the Left is willing to escalate political tensions. Campus politics are no longer about arguments or spirited debates. Left-wing campus activists reject basic American concepts like free speech and due process, and are willing to escalate their "activism" to physical violence. Such attacks used to be fringe incidents when I was an anarchist, and they typically targeted heinous people. Although, even they have the right to free speech. However, after seeing my friend assaulted without justification, I realized I needed to speak out and expose the dangerous movement to which I once belonged.

The Berkeley attack was neither the first nor second time Hayden had been assaulted. It was the third. Just a month earlier, both Hayden and I were attacked by two different students from UCLA. The attacks were more like tantrums than aggravated assaults. But they expose a recurring pattern of left-wing students lashing out against conservatives without just cause. Such a pattern will escalate to full-blown conflict if Americans fail to stop Antifa at its source—college campuses.

From the start of my political career, I wanted to help people. In my youth, I thought that meant breaking many criminal statutes. I felt my cause justified my indiscretions. In my pursuit for equality, I made a lot of mistakes. But I hope that what I learned during that time can finally be used for good.

This book is not an extensive study of the history of Antifa, anarchism, or American radical movements. Such a book would take much time to write, and would require many more pages to do justice to the anarchist tradition.

The purpose of this book is to detail the tactics Antifa currently uses, including some with which I have firsthand experience. My hope is that young people, especially students, who read this book can learn to protect and defend themselves against these tactics. Especially since college administrators often work in tandem with Antifa to violate the rights of conservative students.

Universities are a breeding ground for radical left-wing politics. Antifa's ideology thrives and receives the most ideological support from college professors and administrators. Leftist faculty have a tremendous power to radicalize students. Many of these students are brainwashed to believe that their destiny is to become militant activists and join extremist groups like those affiliated with Antifa.

Antifa is strongly anti-American. However, to say its members are acting only from hate is to oversimplify the movement.

The first few chapters will lay out my experience as an anti-fascist activist, and my transition into the conservative free speech activist I now am. The second explains my background and answers why I joined a movement like antifascism in this first place. The third chapter will give a brief account of Antifa's history, structure, and how I have seen the Antifa network operate.

The second part of the book describes the work I have been doing for the past seven years as a conservative activist. I will also advise on how to combat Antifa while detailing their different strategies. I will further explain how colleges, the mainstream media, and left-wing politicians work to promote Antifa's ideology.

In the last portion of the book, I will take a more ideological tack. While Antifa's tactics are damning, their underlying antifascist argument is worth considering. While ironic when juxtaposed with their tactics, Antifa believes (at least, nominally) in inclusivity and kindness. Thus, the ideological case for left-wing attacks against free speech can often be persuasive. I have read multiple persuasive arguments to ban hate speech. I want to address a few and argue against them. Finally, I will provide some thoughts on how to bridge the political divide in America.

The problem of Antifa and radical politics is a complex issue. But I know we can bridge the partisan divide if we remember one crucial truth: we are all human.

CHAPTER 1

MY TIME AS AN ANTIFASCIST ACTIVIST

I still remember the first time I put on the black mask. It was 2011, in Claremont, California. The rally was intended to fight against the National Socialist Movement (NSM), a neo-Nazi group. The NSM is a white supremacist group that wants a nation in which citizenship is "limited to White persons who share [their] values, and White persons alone."[1] With NSM, unless you are white, you can forget about your civil rights.

I could not believe that in our day and age, hatred like that still existed. As a millennial, racism was foreign to me—an archaic idea that should be lost to time, never to return. It was baffling to me why someone would hate another for being a different color or ethnicity. Yet Nazis marched down the street in my community.

I joined the antifascist movement because it claimed to fight against this type of bigotry, and many Americans can sympathize with its stated mission. This is because America has stood against tyranny since its inception, from fighting a tyrannical Crown in the 1700s, to fighting Nazism in the 1940s, and Communism during the Cold War. While the American government has sometimes failed its people, the American sentiment and identity outwardly rejects fascism and tyranny. In line with this tradition, I identified as a true American antifascist.

I was proud to have worn the black mask. I felt good about standing up for those who were being targeted by the NSM's hateful rhetoric. These racist white supremacists pretend to be American, while they march with swastikas tattooed all over their bodies. They must have forgotten that Americans died fighting against the Nazi regime. Nazism conflicts with basic American principles of freedom and equality. The values of Americans and Nazis cannot logically exist together. Wearing the black bandana made me feel like I was in the front lines to fight a hateful movement before it could spread.

At that moment, I decided I wanted to dedicate my life to protecting others. I wanted to speak for the voiceless, to represent the oppressed, and to fight for what I believed was right. As a teenager, all I wanted was to see justice and fairness. To fight against bigotry and hate so that people "will not be judged by the color of their skin, but by the content of their character," as Dr. Martin Luther King once famously said. And yet there I was, surrounded by Nazis. A common slogan among antifascist activists is "Never Again!" in reference to the atrocities committed against Jews by Nazi Germany. I believed that being part of the antifascist movement meant to never again allow another genocide.

Unfortunately, Antifa is a self-righteous movement, the members of which refuse to see when they become the oppressors. Antifa becomes the same hateful movement it purports to fight against.

I first heard about the Claremont Nazi rally on the news, giving me several weeks to prepare. I complained ad nauseam to my friends about the rally. But the night before the event, I decided to attend. I still believe that if you do not fight for your values, you have none to stand on.

Antifa had already existed around the world for several decades. Yet it rarely received any press coverage. Any time the media took notice, as it did during the famous 1999 World Trade Organization (WTO) riots in Seattle, they would refer to them merely as anarchists. But while there can often be overlap, not all anarchists are part of the antifascist movement, and not all Antifa activists are anarchists.

After the Claremont rally, news coverage showed photos of anarchists displaying flags with the Antifa logo, but I do not recall once hearing or reading the name *Antifa* in any headline. Antifa's obscurity in 2011 is why in 2017, when I attended a march from Oakland to Berkeley, I was surprised to hear a crowd of over two hundred demonstrators chant, "We are Antifa."

Interestingly enough, at this rally, leftist agitator Yvette Felarca confronted my friend Isaac Edikauskas and me. Felarca is a prominent leader of By Any Means Necessary (BAMN), which is a self-proclaimed antifascist organization. While only being a schoolteacher, she has demonstrated her willingness to escalate a situation to physical violence, and has been arrested time and time again for rioting-related charges and for hurting other activists.[2]

During this 2017 rally, Isaac and I were intent on monitoring the march to document any acts of violence against conservative students. We attempted to blend in with the crowd, but Yvette recognized Isaac, as he would routinely help Berkeley conservative students while we both worked for the Leadership Institute.

She began to yell at us as soon as she saw him. The attention we received began to grow, so I suggested we leave before matters escalated.

I first met other Antifa activists at the Claremont for Peace rally held at Memorial Park in Claremont, California. As I walked through the park, a black dog and a white dog were fighting. I took it as an omen of what could follow. I hung out under a tree with my face covered while I scoped out the area, but I saw only hippies and liberals playing music about peace and love. After a while, another activist, who was also in all black, approached me and asked if I wanted to join him and a few others. The plan was to march together to where the Nazis were scheduled to rally. I agreed to join them, but I stayed back until there was a call for us to confront the neo-Nazis. After about twenty minutes, a different activist in a black mask used a megaphone and said, "If you want to actually do something and fight back, follow me." That is when I joined them.

A kind girl gave me a black and red flag. The flag symbolizes many ideologies, but I knew it as the anarcho-collectivist flag, which represents a quasi-socialist ideology that emphasizes anarchism and labor unions. Other people use the flag to represent anarcho-socialism or anarcho-communism. Until that moment, I had only seen that flag in pictures.

Other people carried the same flag, but there were many other flags as well. Among them were the classic anarchist black flag, and one that sported the Antifa logo. Since then, I have seen many other combinations, including black and green, black and purple, and black and gold, which respectively symbolize eco-anarchism, feminist anarchism, and anarcho-capitalism, although the last is widely rejected as being a fake form of anarchism. The only time

I have seen all the flags at the same rally was during the Occupy Wall Street protests. In the end, I felt like I had finally marched with people who shared the same beliefs as me. This was the beginning of my serious leftist activism.

We were not too far from where the neo-Nazis were to meet, but we walked down various alleys to avoid detection. We marched in silence, which was broken by the crisp sound of our footsteps as we marched on wet alleyways. This moment was exhilarating. However, this protest was uneventful since the police set a scrimmage line between the neo-Nazis and other counter-protesters. All that happened was a bunch of names thrown at one another.

The neo-Nazi group was protesting the California Dream Act, which was to give college aid to undocumented immigrants in the state. When someone realized I spoke Spanish, they handed me the megaphone so I could lead some chants in my native language to further annoy the Nazis.

A chant I started was, "Get those animals off those horses," in reference to the horse-mounted officers who were trying to keep the peace.

I also remember an older white woman on our side of the scrimmage line who was uttering statements that appeared to be supportive of the neo-Nazis. A leftist activist was arguing with her, and I heard him say he was part of Anti-Racist Action, another Antifa-type group.

As the argument progressed, I yelled at the police, "People here don't feel safe with her on this side."

Thus, despite it being my first rally, I took an active part in attempts to instigate an altercation.

While there were hundreds of counter-protesters present, there were likely less than fifteen people wearing the black mask, so the media did not take special note of us. I expected as much—*The revolution will not be televised*, as my friends used to say to one another. After the event, I remember going to my favorite Mexican restaurant in my hometown and eating in silence. I was in disbelief that I had stood face-to-face with a bunch of people who wished death upon me simply based on the color of my skin. I was also in disbelief that I stood up to the police. While nothing serious occurred at the rally, I left the demonstration with a new list of contacts that I would put to use in the following year and a half.

To reiterate, not every protest and demonstration I attended as an anarchist was under the banner of Antifa. Antifa is a special movement, and it would be a disservice to claim all anarchists are part of it. In fact, the anarchist Left is a pastiche of loosely over-lapping groups. For example, in 1999, anarchists, socialists, and other left-wing activists conducted a series of protests in Seattle to oppose the WTO.[3] Many anti-capitalism groups were involved. Some were violent, while others attempted to be peaceful. The more violent agitators used the classic "black bloc" strategy, in which they would dress in all-black attire while covering their faces to avoid detection. I have heard many people incorrectly claim that all who wear black clothing at protests are Antifa. The black bloc is merely a tactic employed by Antifa and many other left-wing radical groups. While those protestors likely supported Antifa, and there likely would have been some overlap, Antifa does not cover every group or action in radical politics.

Later that year, I connected with an anarchist in Hollywood who was a prominent member of a local Anonymous group. Inspired by the movie *V for Vendetta*, featuring a faceless terrorist who wears a Guy Fawkes mask. Anonymous is an organization which, much like Antifa, espouses the membership of anyone who shares its values. However, the group is much different, as it is not strictly left wing. For example, libertarians routinely support Anonymous when it fights against government surveillance. Often, Anonymous activism consists of online hacking and doxing, but sometimes the group holds demonstrations. To this day, conservatives, libertarians, and left-wing anarchists alike proudly wear the Guy Fawkes mask.

The Hollywood activist and I corresponded through an encrypted page he set up, but we met only twice in person. Even then, we never saw each other's faces. I found him to be generally unserious. Still, at a Hollywood Walk of Fame demonstration, he did connect me with a younger teenager whom I took under my wing for a while. I must have been seventeen at the time, but this kid was only fourteen, and had been involved in politics for only a few months. While I had only recently been involved with more radical activism, I became politically active around the same age as him. So as an older anarchist, I felt my duty was to pass down the few tactics I had learned from even older anarchists, and I gave him advice on a variety of things.

For example, I taught him the importance of befriending the community. The Hollywood Walk of Fame is replete with cameras from business, tourists, and many other sources. It is also replete with police and security. Therefore, performing left-wing activism in Hollywood came with a heightened danger of being identified, especially since driving would reveal people's license plates, and taking public transportation would help police track down where an activist was headed. To my knowledge, no one was ever tracked down by the police, because these demonstrations were largely peaceful. But we took these precautions in case we found ourselves in a situation in which we needed to flee. So before leaving a demonstration there, we needed to find a place to change our clothes.

The best place I could find was a T-shirt store owned by someone who looked like he hated the government. When we walked in, we must have scared the owner, because we were still wearing bandanas on our faces. But he allowed us to explain ourselves and said that he supported our anti-American activism. He let us change in the store, and even gave us T-shirts so we could avoid further detection.

This may seem like a minor detail, but it is not. A lot of serious left-wing activists are smart enough to know they need to garner support from the general public to survive. Established antifascist activists often have small networks of legitimate businesses they can count on for support.

My left-wing activism was broad. I attended antiwar demonstrations, antipolice gatherings, pro-immigrant rights marches, and, of course, antiracist rallies. But one of my main concerns as an anarchist was animal rights. I was vegetarian for about three years, and vegan for about one and a half, which went on even after I became a libertarian. While I now eat meat, I still find joy in helping animals. My wife and I volunteer to care for homeless cats every weekend. Not to mention the half-dozen dogs I rescued while I lived in California, two of which I helped find their original owners. One, who was missing an eye and had a broken neck and back, I kept and named Pancake. Four years later, he is still alive. That is the type of animal rights activism in which I should have involved myself.

Instead, I thought vandalism helped cows. I remember being fed up with corporate farms. So I did what any "rational" person would do. I left my house around 9:00 p.m., and walked for several hours. I stole someone's bike and rode it for several more hours, until I was in the middle of nowhere in Los Angeles County. That is when I threw rock to smash the window of a McDonald's. As the glass shattered, I hopped on the bike and rode off, then ditched the bike and walked the rest of the way home. This endeavor took several hours. I arrived home around sunrise. Once I got home, I slipped to my room and slept the whole day, feeling a deep sense of accomplishment. Somehow I thought what I had done would cause American capitalism and consumerism to crumble and fall.

I justified my crimes of theft and destruction of property by believing it was a victimless act. The only one being "hurt" was the corporation's bottom line. This dangerous justification of the destruction of property is especially popular among left-wing commentators amid the George Floyd riots. As *New York Times Magazine* reporter Nikole Hannah-Jones said in an interview to CBS News, "Violence is when an agent of the state kneels on a man's neck until all of the life is leached out of his body. Destroying property, which can be replaced, is not violence. To use the same language to describe those two things is not moral."[4]

Of course, the value of a life is much greater than the cost of replacing a window, or even reconstructing a burned-down building. There is no denying that. However, Hannah-Jones's argument is specious and morally bankrupt because the destruction of property does harm human beings, and is considered a violent crime in any other context.

It was not until years later when I talked to my dad about the incident that I realized how harmful it was. He told me that breaking the windows of a business does not hurt the corporation or its shareholders. They probably will never even hear about it—especially since McDonald's is a franchise. Destroying businesses hurts the employees who are forced to go home for the day, which in turn hurts their families because their paycheck is smaller, which translates to fewer groceries. It also hurts the business owner, who is forced to spend hundreds, sometimes thousands, of dollars to fix their establishment. In some cases, it hurts the customers because the business may have to close temporarily and must also increase prices to make up for the damage. And some business owners may never recover from the financial burden placed upon them by left-wing agitators. Destruction of property is not victimless. It hurts real people and real families.

While my broken window may have resulted in a few hundred dollars of damage, other left-wing animal rights activists are willing to go far beyond that. The Animal Liberation Front (ALF) and the Earth Liberation Front (ELF) are avowed ecoterrorist organizations who have perpetrated an unconscionable amount of damage against the livelihoods of thousands. According to the FBI, in a period from 1996 to 2002, the two groups committed over six hundred criminal acts and caused over $46 million in property damage.[5] These ecoterrorists are more criminal than activists. While the threat they once posed has mostly subsided, their extremist ideology is beginning to resurge in American society.

In August 2018, two men entered a family-owned dealership in Fontana, California, and sprayed over a hundred cars with a chemical that destroyed the paint and metal. This act of "activism" caused the family-owned business hundreds of thousands of dollars.[6] While I cannot with certainty claim that the attack was the work of the Earth Liberation Front, the crime fits their profile. It reminds me of when I heard that ELF put sugar into the fuel tanks of cars to destroy them. At the time, such an action was too extreme for me. I knew that the acts of the Animal Liberation Front and the Earth Liberation Front were classified as terrorist acts. Even back then, I wanted nothing to do with terrorist groups.

The two men who sprayed the cars likely thought they were helping the environment. But their "activism" did not help Mother Earth in any way. All they accomplished was to force the family to buy new hoods and use gallons of paint to fix the cars.

Although I was not as extreme as some anarchist I read and heard about, I did other things I now regret.

In one animal rights demonstration, a group of friends and I drove to the home of a corporate CEO. When we arrived, we met about ten to fifteen other people. Some wore the black mask, but others wore plain clothes. I was told we were targeting him because he was the CEO of a company that supposedly had a contract with a French airline. The purpose of the agreement was to transport monkeys to America for animal testing—or so I was told. It is a shame that I never even questioned the motive of the activism. All I did was show up on Sunday and harass the gentleman.

Once outside the home, we shouted obscenities in broad daylight and in front of the neighborhood children.

"You should die!"

"Fascist Pig!"

"Fuck you, you animal killer!"

The list went on. The funny part is, he wasn't even home. The sad part is, we knew that.

The point of us showing up and harassing this guy at his home was not to talk to him and come to an agreement or compromise. Our purpose was to intimidate him and irritate his neighbors. We made sure to polarize the situation so the neighbors understood that if they wanted to get rid of us, they needed to get rid of him. And we gave them good reason to hate him. Not only did we disrupt their Sunday morning, we also made the CEO a villain who tortured innocent monkeys. In effect, this allowed them to feel justified in going against him. We were counting on that when we left, their neighbors would go to his home and demand action. We wanted them to say, *"You need to listen to these people, because we can't take it anymore. We can't have our children learning all these hateful words. If you don't do what they want, we are going to have problems."*

Antifa is not about compromise. That is not how left-wing activism works. Antifa wants victory by any means necessary, and that includes using fear and intimidation.

The strategy we used against the CEO comes straight from Saul Alinsky's *Rules for Radicals*. Alinsky's book, which is cheekily dedicated to Satan, teaches left-wing organizers how to play dirty tricks in pursuit of their goals. The tactic we used is simply a manifestation of Rule 13:

> Pick the target, freeze it, personalize it, and polarize it.
>
> In conflict tactics, there are certain rules that the organizer should always regard as universalities. One is that the opposition must be singled out as the target and "frozen." By this I mean that in a complex, interrelated urban society, it becomes increasingly difficult to single out who is to blame for any particular evil. There is a constant, and somewhat legitimate, passing of the buck. In these times of urbanization, complex metropolitan governments, the complexities of major interlocked corporations, and the interlocking of political life between cities and counties and metropolitan authorities, the problem that threatens to loom more and

more is that of identifying the enemy. Obviously, there is no point to tactics unless one has a target upon which to center the attacks. One big problem is a constant shifting of responsibility from one jurisdiction to another—individuals and bureaus one after another disclaim responsibility for particular conditions, attributing the authority for any change to some other force. In a corporation, one gets the situation where the president of the corporation says that he does not have the responsibility, it is up to the board of trustees, or board of directors, the board of directors can shift it over to the stockholders, etc., etc....

When you freeze the target, you disregard these arguments, and for the moment, all the others to blame.

Then, as you zero in and freeze your target and carry out your attack, all of the "others" come out of the woodwork very soon. They become visible by their support of the target.

The other important point in the choosing of a target is that it must be a personification, not something general and abstract such as a community's segregated practices or a major corporation or City Hall. It is not possible to develop the necessary hostility against, say, City Hall, which after all is a concrete, physical, inanimate structure, or against a corporation, which has no soul or identity, or a public-school administration, which again is an inanimate system....

With this focus comes a polarization. As we have indicated before, all issues must be polarized if action is to follow.[7]

The rule is simple. People do not care about complex issues. There needs to be a human component, something relatable which people can champion, and an enemy to vilify. We used this tactic on this CEO. We did not allow him to pass the buck or get away by blaming others. We forced him to own the responsibility to act. We froze him and made sure people understood that he was responsible for torturing animals, even if that statement was false. His guilt or innocence was immaterial.

This tactic is not used only by violent agitators. It is such a powerful tool that it permeates mainstream American politics. Often left-wing politicians and activists use this tactic to attack Jeff Bezos and Amazon. Jeff Bezos created an incredible service that millions upon millions of people benefit from. Yet ask any radical leftist who is to blame for people starving, and many will quickly say billionaires. Ask for a specific example, and many of them accuse Jeff Bezos for earning so much money while his workers earn pennies.

Of course, the Left goes after Bezos and not Amazon because if they attacked Amazon, they would garner little to no support. First, as Alinsky would say, Amazon is a corporation with no soul or identity. It is incredibly difficult, almost impossible, to convince people to hate the service. But second, Amazon is such a great service that people would not be able to understand why it is evil. Instead, left-wing activists attack Jeff Bezos, the richest man on earth, because he is the personification of rich and greedy white men. They freeze him and blame him for poverty, when he employees thousands upon thousands of people, doing more for them than any government could.

Former Nevada Democratic Senator Harry Reid used this tactic to fight against conservative money in politics.[8] Political donations are a complex issue and it may take years to understand how to comply with American election rules. As Alinsky says, the problem is too complicated for most people to understand. Instead of debating and compromising on this issue,

Senator Reid would take to the Senate floor to defame the Koch brothers and proclaim they were "at it again" for donating to his political opponents. He gave Democrats and the Left a target to fight against—"big money" in politics—as if they were the only ones exercising their First Amendment rights.

Unsurprisingly, during the 2016 election, the biggest donor was a democratic supporter, who gave $91,078,136 to democrats and liberals.[9] That amount is almost $10 million more than the next biggest donor. Charles Koch is the fifty-fifth largest donor on the list, and he donated around $80 million less than the leading democrat. Charles Koch did give large amounts of money to his preferred candidates, but Harry Reid's claims are unfounded. The Koch brothers were not trying to buy elections; they were simply doing what everyone from both sides of the aisle are doing—donating to causes and candidates in which they believe. Unfortunately, Harry Reid's slander overshadowed the millions of dollars the Koch brothers donate to charities. So when David Koch passed away in 2019, democrats all over the country wrongly rejoiced.[10]

As mentioned earlier, I was an anarcho-punk, which means I attended many gigs where music groups would play. I enjoyed these shows, and I also played in a few bands as a guitarist and sometimes vocalist. But most of the time, I took the opportunity to sell my homemade merchandise.

At first, I made stencils of band logos or political statements out of cereal boxes, and used spray paint to print them onto fabric to make patches. But I soon bought a silk-screen press and cranked up production. After a few months, I established a DIY distro with the help of a couple friends.

At one point, the operation grew big enough to take large orders from bands, on demand. I also used to dumpster dive with friends to find more things to sell. Our favorite hunting ground was in the mall in West Covina. There are many companies who throw away good merchandise—including Hot Topic. Since we had a friend who worked at one of the restaurants, she had access to the dumpsters. In one haul, we managed to take home several new items, including Doc Marten boots, dresses, T-shirts, and other accessories. We had bins full of thousands of dollars' worth of merchandise. Yet we sold the items cheap because, for us, it was never about the money. The distro was merely a means to fund our activism.

While some of the money was reinvested in making more merchandise, most went to buying ink and paper so I could print zines and newsletters, which I circulated at the same shows where I sold merchandise. Some of the newsletters promoted conspiracy theories, such as false information about how some street light cameras appeared to be pointed at homes, suggesting government surveillance. In another, I argued that President Obama and Secretary of State Clinton wanted to declare martial law. Yet somehow I managed to get people to read them and believe them.

In the end, the distro was highly successful, because even though we had to invest our own money, I was able to convince more people to join the antifascist movement.

I now find it insane how fast my network grew in such a short time. When I first attended the Claremont rally, I did not know who I was going to meet. Now, people in my network were routinely active all throughout Southern California. We attended numerous protests together, including the Occupy protests in Los Angeles, as well as doing independent activism.

However, there was another event to which we all particularly looked forward, namely the return of the National Socialist Movement. This time, they were gathering in Pomona. While Pomona is immediately west of Claremont, it has many more Hispanic residents, so we expected a much larger counterprotest.

Before Claremont, I knew no one in the movement. Only a few months later, twenty antifascist activists were waiting for me to drive them to Pomona. I bought black fabric to make an anarchist flag for the rally. I also bought a large wooden pole to fly it, and which I could also use to defend myself if things got ugly.

When I arrived at the apartment where people were waiting, some were joking around while others strategized an entrance and exit strategy. Meanwhile, I sat on the floor and hurried to stitch the flag together. I was the youngest in the group, but I was proud to be able to get some people to join in, who would otherwise not have. I considered it a badge of honor to help grow the radical leftist movement.

The first thing we needed to decide was how to get to Pomona. We checked to see who had cars and was willing to drive. Once we made sure everyone had transportation, we discussed a means to get out. The plan was to park in a secluded area, close by, but not in the weeds of the protest. Ideally, a place that was either residential or covered by trees, where we could leave the cars without arousing suspicion. At the very least, it should be a location where we knew the businesses or residents would be reluctant to hand over surveillance tapes to the police.

Funny enough, while we separated into groups, most of us ended up parking in the same place—near a rundown business. We figured there would be no cameras nearby, and the rundown cars blended with other cars similarly parked. Once we arrived, we regrouped and marched together toward Pomona City Hall.

This rally felt different from the Claremont affair. When we arrived, we were surrounded by journalists who took pictures of us marching. This time, the black bloc looked menacing. A friend of mine grabbed the interest of the media because he paraded an upside-down American flag with the circled-A anarchist symbol and other anti-American insignia. The journalists also took a special interest in me because I was one of the few who marched with a flag. As we marched, we joined dozens of other counter-protesters already there.

It didn't take long for riot police from different cities around Los Angeles and San Bernardino County to surround us. Multiple Antifa activists started yelling at the police, telling them to "do the right thing" and go home, and that we would "take care" of the neo-Nazis. When the police stayed silent, the anarchists grew belligerent and began accusing them of being white supremacists who agreed with the neo-Nazis. As for the Hispanic and African-American officers, the left-wing radicals called them race traitors.

I had no intent to get into a physical altercation at that protest. Still, I knew that if the situation called for it, I was expected to be part of the fight.

When the Nazis came into view, they were being escorted by the police. We all ran toward them as I waved the black flag high. We were in front of their noses. There was little separating us from the white supremacists, and we severely outnumbered them. Antifa began throwing rocks, traffic cones and other projectiles at the white supremacists, but the cops used their shields to deflect them. Luckily for everyone, the police intercepted us and created a scrimmage line between the two groups. At first, many of us were hesitant. Some people began inching closer to the cops as harsh words were exchanged. Then officers on horseback trotted in and forced us to retreat across the street. Officers mounted on horses are typically used in these types of demonstrations because they allow police officers to move swiftly to create divides among the demonstrators without posing great danger to them.

As tensions swelled, another activist and I tried climbing a structure on our side of the street, but an officer threatened to arrest us if we did not climb down. I complied because there were still not enough counter-protesters in the black bloc for us to avoid arrests. Once I returned to the ground, I ran back and forth on the sidewalk to start chants against the neo-Nazis. Eventually, people began throwing tortillas to further infuriate them. Yet nothing significant happened for most of the event. The National Socialist Movement leader delivered a speech, and that was that.

But what I found most troubling at the time was that the police line faced us and not the neo-Nazis. Their actions only reinforced my belief that the police were in bed with the fascists. Unfortunately, I failed to understand that there are competing rights and interests in America, and the police were there to protect the rights of everyone, including those I deemed hateful. If they refuse to do so, their act establishes a precedent whereby the government can begin censoring legitimate speech it does not like.

Even though nothing significant happened during the rally, the number of counterprotestors dramatically increased, and we felt more and more emboldened. As the rally neared its end, the situation quickly deteriorated. As the neo-Nazis began retreating, we broke through the police lines and ran after them. I took down a police barricade to make sure the people behind me were not slowed down. The rally began to veer into a riot.

Recklessly, we followed the neo-Nazis until they barricaded themselves inside a quad, which was covered by walls, but without a roof. Yielding under pressure from police, some protesters backed off, but others threw rocks over the walls, while many attempted to jump over. At that point, the police began to take a more hands-on approach, and confronted the antifascist demonstrators. Now more emboldened, the neo-Nazis started shouting back at us through the gates while they hid behind police officers who were ready to arrest anyone who came in.

I wanted to do more than yell, so I tried to break down one of the gates. As soon as police officers saw me, they hit the barrier with their riot batons to ward me off. The police on horseback ran through the crowd to defend the gate and disperse the crowd. A friend of mine saw the horses galloping, so he put his arms around me and pulled me away. I had not seen the officer coming, and had my friend not done that, I would have been caught and arrested.

Finally, the white supremacists drove off while recording their exit. Similarly, many Antifa activists took pictures of their license plates. Those pictures would be used to identify and dox them to their employers. Now that the main event was over, we realized we needed to go. Many of us split up and went to different locations. Some of them I never saw again. Others, I have randomly run into on the streets.

This rally is one of the last significant protests I attended, and it marked a turning point in my time as a radical activist. For some time after that, I attended activist events and anarchist meetups. But that was the last time I was part of the black bloc and put on the black mask. Although I had been a left-wing activist since 2009, my involvement with Antifa was brief, spanning from early

2011 to mid-2012. Fortunately, throughout my time with Antifa, I never physically hurt another person.

After all this chaos, I grew increasingly paranoid, so I withdrew from my hard anarchist activism. Instead, I focused on recruiting other people to replace me. I thought it would be more fruitful if I could find others to break windows.

To find more activists, I started writing a lot more zines and passed them around in different venues. I did not do any significant activism at the time. However, the anarchist cause was important enough for me to continue to spread the word.

* * *

In 2011, I took my first American government class. The course mainly focused on the American constitutional system, but also looked at political ideologies in general. The teacher, Mr. Darren Near, was a passionate man, which led many people to find him intimidating. However, he merely wanted to instill the value of being involved in politics in each of his pupils. He was a conservative person and often discussed current events, including the 2012 Republican presidential primary, and gave his opinion on each of the candidates. While he was open about his opinion, he was also fair to his students, and he never belittled anyone.

I found his class interesting, but as a left-wing anarchist, I did not believe government was capable of solving social problems. Instead, I believed that people working collectively could work to abolish private property and the oppressive hierarchy of capitalism.

I started my first economics class the next semester with, again, a conservative teacher. Mr. Cliff Korzep is one of the most influential teachers I had while at Azusa High School. He was a former Marine who towered over students with impressive height. Many students found him intimidating as well because he was a serious person, but he was also incredibly kind. Surprisingly, there were more than two conservative teachers at my school. But their behavior was strikingly different from that of their liberal peers. Liberal teachers were often out front and center belittling conservative thought. For their part, the conservative teachers were open to being criticized, and approached learning in a spirit of curiosity.

My economics class was far more enjoyable than the American government course. Mr. Korzep was the first to introduce me to Keynesian and laissez-faire economics. The economic theory developed by John Maynard Keynes, which proposes that government intervention can stabilize the economy, did not appeal to me at all. It sounded like a justification for big government, and as an anarchist, I was suspicious of all forms of authority. Laissez-faire economics proposes a hands-off approach to the economy, and believes people are better positioned to invest in their futures than government. As an individualist, I found this theory more attractive.

I learned more about the free market when I stumbled upon Milton Friedman and Thomas Sowell, two great modern economic minds who argued that government often creates more problems than it solves. I would often read their papers and articles, or watch YouTube videos about them, and wrestle with their ideas in my head.

One concept often brought up by free-market economists is the tragedy of the commons. This idea proposes that one does not have an incentive to care for land that is not his own. Instead, the average person is naturally incentivized to plunder the land for all the resources it has to offer, thereby destroying the land entirely. The solution, according to free-marketeers, is to allow people to own property because they will then be more incentivized to care of it and not allow it to decay. This idea conflicts with the left-wing notion of land ownership. According to many leftists, owning land is stealing. According to their reasoning, we do not own the earth; we share the world with everyone.

When I first learned about the tragedy of the commons, I was hooked. But then I found that it is a principle used not only in economics, but also in nature. This forced me to reassess my beliefs.

Anarchists and socialists do make a distinction between personal and real property. For example, they would concede the idea of owning a toothbrush or a car. But the problem with socialist economics, as Friedman and Sowell would argue, is that personal property does not come out of thin air. Goods are created because of the ingenuity of people who are incentivized under a free enterprise system. Without the free market, as the libertarians argue, there is no wealth to redistribute. This idea was strange to me at first, but it then began to make sense.

However, I am a stubborn person. So I was not going to accept the ideas willingly. I wanted to disprove the free market. I began by reading more leftist materials, including a book called *The Accumulation of Freedom: Writings on Anarchist Economics,* published by the leftist AK Press.[11] The book purports to be the answer to capitalism and the free market. Yet as I read each page, I often found strawman arguments. To quote an introductory passage:

> Capitalism is a resilient system, oftentimes changing features in reaction to class struggle as well as its own internal

limitations. As opponents of capitalism, then, anarchists have been concerned not just with describing capitalism as it is, but also as it may be. That is, if we want to move beyond capitalism to something altogether different, then we need to understand how capitalism can recuperate struggles that seem at first glance to develop in opposition to it. This means attempting to analyze how capitalism has changed, and might change, in order to satisfy popular demands and still allow for the continuation of capital accumulation despite resistance to the system.[12]

In March 2020, due to the coronavirus lockdowns, my wife and I drove to my parents' house in California. I took the opportunity to look through my old literature, and I found my original copy of this book. On this page, right next to the quote above, I wrote in 2012, "Doesn't this paragraph prove the free hand of the market correct?" The author's tone leads one to believe that capitalism is a system which was imposed on the people. The line shows complete misunderstanding of the free market. Capitalism is not a system imposed on people; capitalism is a hands-off system in which the government is supposed to get out of the way in most of the economy. Capitalism does not change. The demands of people in a free society change. In a free society, if there was a better system than capitalism, people would naturally demand it in mass as opposed to being forced to participate, as so many socialist governments have demonstrated.[13]

I also picked up *Downsizing the Federal Government* by Chris Edwards of the Cato Institute, and it contained persuasive examples and statistics of why free-market policies work.[14] I could not find radical left-wing books as persuasive and sophisticated as Edwards's. Left-wing books provided me with no good answers, so I moved on from books and talked to the left-wing activists themselves. That was the first time someone called me a capitalist pig—simply for asking questions. I wanted to find a reason to believe in anarchism, but sadly found most so-called anarchists to be socialists or communists. They did not hate authority as I did. They wanted to use the power of the state to do their bidding, while pretending to fight for the oppressed.

A conversation with another radical activist will forever be ingrained in my memory. The subject was the role of government in our society. I told this person that I did not believe in government, and that government was the cause of many of today's problems. I argued that if a government is to exist, it should be present only in small doses, mainly to protect people's rights. This person's response opened my eyes to what a farce many so-called anarchists were.

He responded, "I don't believe in government, but if the government is to exist, it should be there to help everyone."

What he was saying was that he, like me, distrusted and despised the government. Yet if a government is to exist, he wanted to give bureaucrats a massive amount of power. If the goal is to have the government take care of everyone, it necessarily needs to be an enormous bureaucracy. Additionally, since everything the government does is backed with force, he wanted to create a totalitarian government, falsely believing that it would not turn against its people. As a so-called anarchist, he loved big government.

In the fall of 2019, I spoke at a fundraiser in Sacramento to help some conservative students. After my remarks, an older gentleman approached me and we conversed for some time. What he told me was heartbreaking. According to him, his brother was devastated because his daughter, who he sent to school in Portland, Oregon, had joined Rose City Antifa. She threatened to stop talking to him unless he stopped posting pro-Trump memes on Facebook. Her father thought it was a bluff, but she made good on her promise.

I had no personal connection to any of the anarchists, so I could easily stop talking to them. However, I cannot imagine how a daughter can stop talking to her own father, who raised her and sent her to college to get a decent education. Family means nothing to some members of the antifascist movement if those family members support the conservative cause.

My last interaction with many of my former friends was some time during my first year of college, at a crust-punk show. The gig featured many bands in which my friends were playing. In total, there must have been around twenty to thirty of my friends present at the event. The show was like any other music gig. While different bands played, the main attractions for many were drugs, sex, and alcohol, often indulged in by those who were underage. Unfortunately, this is the type of behavior that attracts many Antifa types.

Amid the chaos, a couple lovebirds were committing a lewd act in the "pee corner." Often, at backyard gigs, the pee corner is just any corner that is away from main "stage," where bands are playing. I have no idea why anyone would think that place to be an appropriate location for engaging in sexual relations, especially with the typical foul smell that accompanies it.

Upon seeing the couple, I made sure to avoid that location. But not long after, the owner of the home, a gang-related individual, arrived to break up the intercourse. I watched this altercation from across the lawn. I did not want to get involved. But I then saw one of my friends attempt to break up the fight. I ran to pull him away because I thought he did not see what had started it. He considered himself a pacifist, so I thought he just wanted to de-escalate the situation. That's when I realized that the couple having sex in public were also my friends.

Next thing I knew, a tall, fat cholo jerked my arm, turned me around, and shouted at me to leave. I put my hands up to create some distance between us, but he responded, "Don't touch me!" He grew more aggressive with each passing second. I knew I was about to get punched in the face. But just before he squared up to me, the first fight broke out two feet away. That drew his attention and allowed me to run toward the crowd, where I started grabbing all our friends for help. Fights broke out across the backyard until many of us made it outside. At one point, I was caught in a head-lock and taken to the ground while multiple *cholos* stomped and kicked me. Luckily, I was able to break free and distance myself from the fray.

I don't remember being stomped. It must have been adren-aline that blocked the pain. I realized I had taken several blows only when several people later said they saw me on the ground. The next day, I had bruises all over my body.

Not every person I grabbed jumped in the fight. And since the home belonged to someone who was gang affiliated, we were severely outnumbered. That rumble was not one we were going to win.

In another instance, I saw a guy on our side being beaten with a gas can as blood poured from his face and skull. He was the hero of the night because he knew only one person in our group, but he fought almost every cholo in sight. As I circled the fights, I began picking up box cutters and screwdrivers that *cholos* had dropped.

I thought, *If I have this, they can't use it against us.* Ultimately, multiple fights broke out across the entire block.

Finally, the police arrived. We were treated to the gang unit, K-9, and a police chopper that monitored the situation. That is when everyone scattered.

I ran to my car and lay low for a few minutes, before I started the car and began picking people up and taking them to another location. Once we were all accounted for, we rested in the garage of a friend's house. Many of us were tired and battered. Then the thought hit me: *I do not want this lifestyle. I do not want the chaos. I want to live in peace.* That night was the last time I saw many of these people.

Antifascist activists claim they want to create an alternative to modern society. One that is above hatred, violence, and chaos. Yet when you look around, they have created a mirror image of the society they claim to despise.

I wanted out. Luckily, I had recently begun studying at Citrus College, which is the local community college near my hometown in Azusa. The school is not exceptional, and it is small by California standards, but it presented an opportunity to escape my past and begin a new experience by meeting new people. At Citrus College, I finally had the opportunity to search for ideas I could believe in.

It is important to note that at this point in my life, I was not a conservative. Even in college, political affiliation tests still placed me on the anarchist left. However, I did have a lot of questions about libertarianism and conservatism. And since all I had found on the Left was violence and intimidation, I began reaching out to the Right.

Finding conservatives on college campuses was not easy at first. Before then, I had never met anyone who openly supported these values, as even the conservative teachers I had in high school never spoke openly about their views in the classroom. I had to resort to the internet for answers. I went online and read as many articles as I could. I also requested information from various conservative organizations. Unfortunately, no one replied. That is, until Adam Weinberg from the Leadership Institute reached out. Adam wanted to meet me in person, and asked if I wanted to start a club on my campus. I do not know if he knew I was a leftist, but I do believe he knew I was not a libertarian. Adam taught me how to "table" and talk to strangers about politics to recruit them. He helped me expand my personal network within the liberty movement. That is when I first realized that conservatives are often hiding on college campuses.

The first time Adam and I went on campus together, he brought along one of his students from Pomona to show me that libertarians do exist. This gentleman was an Iraq war veteran who had lost an arm in battle. I was too timid to ask him about it, but he and Adam both told me about their experiences in pro-liberty activism. I listened carefully, and the discussion was not ideological, but tactical. Adam taught me how to talk to passersby about politics—an incredibly difficult task. Politics is boring. To get someone engaged, you must have a great pitch. Luckily, Adam did. "Do you like liberty?" is still a line I use when recruiting students on college campuses.

We did this for about an hour, and to my surprise, we signed up over fifty people. I was beginning to feel great about starting this club, when my first interaction with the Left occurred.

A maintenance worker passed our table and yelled, "We could use those signs for the union."

The comment was not rude in itself, nor anything close to intimidation. Ironically, I still supported unions at the time. However, this brief interaction did foreshadow the type of anti-conservative bias I would experience during my time at Citrus College.

Adam told me that from time to time I would experience some crazies, but not to let that drag me down. I just needed to keep my head up and continue talking to students. And physical violence against conservative students was not as common then as it is today. Neither Adam nor I knew that physical violence would soon escalate on campuses across the country. We certainly never expected that the violent tactics pioneered on college campuses would spread across dozens of American cities while left-wing politicians and their media allies alternately praised Antifa and denied its existence.

Adam recommended books to read, like Frédéric Bastiat's *The Law*, and I made it required reading for my first meeting. Bastiat argues that all law is force, and that while force is justified in self-defense, force as an aggressor is not warranted. Thus, the government is justified when they write laws to collectively defend the rights of people. However, some laws turn the government into the aggressor, and thus are immoral.[15] He called this "legal plunder," and it manifests when the government gives special rights to certain groups, but not to others. He argued that just because something is legal does not mean it is moral. Although the book did not have numbers and statistics, Bastiat used simple, concise, and almost infallible logic. Frédéric Bastiat's *The Law* is one of the most important books I have ever read, and it contains fewer than twenty thousand words—about a third the size of this book.

Adam and I also talked about the issues of the day and had many conversations about the meaning of living free. When I talked to my leftist friends and played devil's advocate, I was called a capitalist pig. In our conversations, I often came at Adam from the Left. But he never once called me a communist pig. Instead, when I challenged his beliefs, he took the time to consider them. Then he would say something like, "Well, that's interesting, but have you ever thought about this…?" or "Have you thought about that?" This was the type of interaction I had been looking for all along. I wanted someone to engage me in debate, dialogue, and conversation.

Adam was a regional field coordinator for the Leadership Institute at the time. A few years after I became conservative, I was hired for Adam's position. A regional field coordinator's responsibility is to help conservative students start their own organizations. We find conservative students and show them that they are not alone on campus. Adam organized conservative students throughout California and several other states. With Adam's help, I decided to start a Young Americans for Liberty (YAL) chapter. The reason I started a libertarian club instead of a general political club was that I wanted to meet more conservative and libertarian students. I found libertarian ideas interesting. I knew that a generic political club would attract only liberals since conservative students often hide their political beliefs. But with Adam's help, I was able to form this club and meet people who disagreed with me.

It took time to find people who were interested in right-wing politics. I called each person on the list, as Adam suggested, to invite them to our first meeting. This was tragically painful for me, as my phone anxiety was much worse than it is today. Since this incident, I have forced myself to call thousands of people, either through my job or phone banking, in campaigns. Yet at the time, every number was more painful than the last. I remember lying in bed with my feet in the air, hoping no one would answer. Yet about ten people did, and said they would attend.

Unfortunately, the day of the meeting only saw three other people, plus my faculty advisor. To make matters worse, I made everyone sit in painful silence for ten minutes as I waited for more people to come through the door.

When I finally started, I felt discouraged, especially when the only girl I recruited walked out mid-meeting. But I knew politics was hard to talk about, so I decided to press on. I told people what the group Young Americans for Liberty was all about, and how we could all get involved, as I gathered them around my tiny laptop screen. In the end, the meeting went exactly as I thought it would—a failure. I ended the meeting half an hour early, and my advisor, a self-described communitarian, was nice enough to give me some tips for the next event.

I was ready to give up. I thought that libertarians and conservatives on campus were not willing to put themselves out there. As I was packing up my laptop and other things, Vincenzo Sinapi-Riddle and one of his friends came through the door, asking whether the meeting was still happening. I remember being delighted at that, and what made me even happier was that he said he wanted a leadership position. I began to believe that the club was going to be a success.

Vinny is a hardcore libertarian. He has been exposed to conservative and libertarian ideas since he was young. But the best part is that he is hilarious. Vinny and I eventually became close friends. But more importantly, he is a huge reason why I became libertarian.

Vinny and I and a few others often went to a small burger joint across the street from Citrus College. I was still vegan at the time, but it was fun to just hang out. The coolest part about this was that we seldom spoke politics at these gatherings. Instead, Vinny and I would just make jokes about our professors or other random subjects. Today, even though I wish I could, I cannot imagine myself having coffee with a leftist student, and I have experienced the disdain some left-wing students feel against conservatives.

For example, on November 2019, I spoke at Emerson College in Boston. I had extra time before the event, so the students invited me to their cafeteria. There were a variety of foods, and it was all you can eat. While the students were in a corner recruiting for my speaking event, I went to order some food. I decided to ask a student for help in ordering since the line was not readily apparent. Thereafter, I struck up a brief conversation with this young man. He asked me if I was a student, and I responded, "No." He then asked me what I was doing on campus.

I pointed to the conservative students. "I'm actually speaking tonight to that group over there."

"Oh…" He walked away from me, abandoning the food he had ordered.

It is a sad state of affairs that conservatives and liberals seem no longer to be able to eat together. When people talk about the good times in college, I remember the days Vinny and I just hung around and cracked jokes at one another, not the times I argued with others about politics.

Nevertheless, Vinny and I did talk a lot about politics. He was the first to introduce me to political theorists like Ludwig von

Mises and Friedrich Hayek. Thus, a combination of friendship and philosophy is what helped craft my political views. Human experience is what truly shapes values and beliefs, which in turn shape political ideology. People do not simply read *The Communist Manifesto* and turn Communist, or read *The Wealth of Nations* and turn libertarian. Ideology is largely based on experience. It was Vinny's friendship that first helped me keep an open mind, but it was because of the persuasive logic of these writers that I began to believe in libertarian economics.

Unfortunately, my friendship with Vinny gave me a false sense of security. I started the YAL chapter during my second semester in college, and I was ecstatic. I thought I was going to find more people like Vinny, both on the Right and the Left. My goal was to talk to people from all sides and debate open-minded individuals about the best way to build a peaceful and prosperous society. I thought that in college I would finally have that opportunity.

I could not have been more wrong.

As soon as people found out I was part of Young Americans for Liberty, they voiced hatred for the club and for me. We experienced liberal bias, and I did not understand why. All I knew was the administration kept working against us. We lost our advisor more than once through the interference of leftist administrators.

I remember being on the campus quad and seeing the student government's advisor talking to my club's faculty advisor. As I approached, the student government advisor walked away, and my advisor said he could no longer advise us because of the activism we were doing. He had been informed that we were ruining his reputation. He had become our advisor as a favor, but in the end, he did not believe what Young Americans for Liberty preached. Thus, he was easily persuaded to abandon us.

Unfortunately, this problem was not unique to us. When I worked as a regional field coordinator, I helped countless students find advisors, but more importantly, to keep them. Time and time again, conservative students ask me how to find an advisor. Sometimes we are successful, but most often I advise them to work as unrecognized student groups because finding an advisor can take months, and they will likely miss their opportunity to promote their ideas if they decide to wait.

The most inspiring story I can think of comes from a Long Beach City College Turning Point USA club I helped. Along with my other Southern California field representative and Turning Point USA staff, I helped create this group and gave it all the resources we had. And for their first event, I called in a favor from a San-Diego-County-based pro-Second Amendment nonprofit, and invited its president to speak on campus.

I was terrified that since this event was the group's first, it would fail, just like my own first meeting. To make matters worse, the room was locked until minutes before the event. As soon as a security officer opened the door, I rushed in and frantically rearranged the chairs so it did not look like a classroom, but an auditorium. In the end, I did not finish in time. Still, almost forty people showed up.

More impressively, a reporter from the school paper was in attendance, along with some student government officers. Even more outstanding was that everyone was engaged and respectful. But most inspiring was the paper's headline the next day: "Conservative Voices Needed at LBCC" (a picture of a MAGA hat on a pile of books accompanied the article).[16]

This event was pure success from start to finish. But the best part came after the article was published. After weeks of asking both liberal and conservative professors to advise the club, the students were now forced to turn down requests to be their advisor. One student later told me that the school was now more open to debates and discussions with conservative thinkers—something almost unheard of on other campuses.

My group was fortunate to find our last advisor because he was also libertarian. Even though he was merely an adjunct professor, he never let us down. Unfortunately, he was like a lone blade of grass in the desert. While we did know of some other conservative professors, almost none of them were willing to stick out their neck like he did, and I do not blame them. Unlike LBCC, Citrus College actively encouraged anticonservative ideas and attitudes.

One of the most discouraging events at Citrus College featured Dolores Huerta during Hispanic Heritage month. Ms. Huerta is not a household name, but she should be. She was the righthand woman to labor organizer César Chávez during the farm worker strikes of previous decades. She has a fantastic leftist political mind that is envied by many. During her speech, she recounted the time she met President Barack Obama and he confessed that he had stolen her line, *Sí se puede*, and changed it to *Yes We Can*.

As a member of the student government, I was tasked with inviting people to the event. I was excited to meet Ms. Huerta because I had read and learned so much about her struggles as an activist. When I was in middle school, I had a teacher whose family lived in the farming camps, and her dad often heard Chávez's speeches. Although she never opined directly, she would quote her dad about Chávez being a man of reason. Additionally, my school made farm workers' stories required reading as part of our study of California history.

In short, I had a positive view of Huerta, and I was not alone. For this event, we expected only about a hundred students, but a crowd of five hundred showed up—there would have been more, but the Campus Center building was at max capacity.

But my perception of Huerta changed as soon as she started talking. She, like so many other leftist activists, promoted an us-versus-them mentality, attacking and berating conservatives while proclaiming that liberals were the true saviors of society. Her most astonishing line was when she called conservatives and Tea Party supporters white racists. According to her, conservatives were all white and stupid because, as everyone knows, everyone descends from Africa and has black blood inside them. I quietly shrieked at that statement. In my group, only one person was white—and he was only half-white. Even if I had objected, I would have been drowned out by the thunderous applause she received. After the event, the student government advisor told me they'd spent $3,000 to get her on campus.

That is not the only time Citrus College promoted anti-American events. Another annual event that Citrus spent thousands hosting was titled, *Celebrating Genocide: Holidays and Mascots in the Colonizing of America*. Dr. Brian Burkhart, an assistant professor and director of American Indian studies at CSU Northridge, was the keynote speaker. The event began with a ritualistic Native American drum session. As soon as Dr. Burkhart began speaking, the anti-American propaganda began to flow. He criticized people he disagreed with, and went on to compare America to the show *Game of Thrones*, to much laughter around the room.

Even though Vinny and I pushed for conservative events, I remember Citrus hosting only one semiconservative event every year—on Constitution Day. Every September 17th, Citrus was federally mandated to host a pro-Constitution event, which they often outsourced to someone who cared. The professor who did was merely an adjunct lecturer, but he took the time to invite conservative and liberal speakers to a debate. I am certain that, were it not for this professor, Citrus would have merely passed out a flyer about the Constitution and called it a day. Yet this professor invited some great commentators, like Ben Shapiro. Ben's honorarium was only $3,000, but rest assured, Citrus College did not pay a cent. Young Americans Foundation picked up the tab.

I remember hearing Ben speak for the first time. The debate dealt with the National Security Agency's newly discovered power to spy on American citizens. Ben spoke second, and he opened with the line, "It's nice to see the other side of the aisle finally begin to worry about government overreach."

Now, Vinny and I were huge Shapiro nerds. Any time we made a "drop the mic" type of joke or argument, we would say, "You just got Shapiroed!" Yet this event occurred in 2013, before Ben attained the national platform he now enjoys, so only about thirty people were present. To make matters worse, almost half of them were forced to be there because they were part of student government.

Nothing Ben said that day was truly controversial, yet being conservative on campus is controversial enough for many on the Left, and even in that half-empty room, you could hear liberal students complaining. On college campuses, you can invite extreme leftist activists and thinkers and receive praise. But if someone goes on stage to criticize President Obama's illegal spying program, as Ben did, people lose their minds.

To be fair, not all the activism my club did was serious. However, some projects touched on important topics. Our first initiative was to gather signatures for a petition to convince the student government to condemn the NSA's practice of surveilling American citizens. Since I was part of student government, I tried to convince my colleagues to vote for the resolution. Moments before we all heard Ben speak on this subject, the student government voted against it. This initiative was also the beginning of the school's escalation of their anticonservative bias against us. One of our best recruiters was Vinny, who got hundreds of signatures all by himself. But when he approached a guy who was sitting in an open field, an administrator rushed out of his building and threatened to kick him off campus for petitioning outside the recognized speech zone.

Colleges like to claim that free speech zones help them advance their educational mission. But in practice, they are often an excuse to confine conservative speech. Vinny's petitioning was done in an open field and over fifty feet away from the nearest classroom. If there was any disruption to educational activities, it was the administrator who tried to enforce the school's unconstitutional policy. Some schools enforce these rules to explicitly disadvantage conservatives. At Georgia Gwinnett College, Chike Uzuegbunam, a Christian student, wanted to share his beliefs on campus by passing out pamphlets.[17] Even though Chike complied with the school's confined speech policies, some students complained to the administration, which labeled his speech "disorderly conduct." Unfortunately, college administrators throughout America routinely use such policies to violate the rights of conservative students.

At Transylvania University in Kentucky, the administration allowed the socialist club to set up shop without permission.

But when a YAF chapter attempted to do the same, they were threatened with sanctions.[18] Transylvania is a private school, so in fairness, it can do what it wants. Even so, it would be content-based discrimination and an unequal enforcement of the contract it signed with the students. Thus, there is some potential liability. Nonetheless, Transylvania's blatant disregard for conservative thought is but a single instance among countless others.

My club faced similar pushback, but we didn't hesitate to voice our grievances. For example, when the student government passed legislation we did not like, we protested. These protests were of no consequence outside of campus. However, there was one incident that the school escalated. On this occasion, we printed a large picture I found online of a communist depiction of a My Little Pony character, and imposed the student government logo underneath, along with the line, "Resist at All Costs," in a Russianesque font. The image was obviously meant to be a parody. Still, many students took issue with the cartoon.

The My Little Pony depiction was apparently a bridge too far, as it prompted the student life advisor to confront us. She was the same one who had talked to our first advisor right before we lost him. As she approached, I grew nervous. She came within earshot of us and began to take pictures of the project.

Nervously, I walked over. "Pretty funny, huh?"

She replied, "We'll see what the lawyers have to say about this."

She was threatening to sue us.

I panicked, and to scare her I said we would call our own lawyers. This statement was a lie. We had no lawyer to defend us. My mind scrambled to think of someone who could help, but I drew a blank. I thought I was going to be forced to spend thousands of dollars to hire an attorney. While I knew the First

Amendment protected my speech, I sure did not feel protected at that moment.

I went to class about half an hour after this incident, but instead of paying attention, I was on my phone getting acquainted with copyright law. I also messaged one of my friends whose dad was a copyright attorney, but she said he would not be able to help.

In this class, the president of the student government was sitting a few rows behind me when the student government advisor walked in and called him outside. After class, he pulled me and my friends aside and told us we were going to be fine because they had forgotten to trademark their own logo.

That is when we realized they wanted us out. Our activism was no longer about losing an advisor, or having trouble getting permission to do activism. They wanted to escalate the situation to suppress our speech. They were willing to use the arm of the state to get their way. So we decided to file a lawsuit against every administrator who had violated our First Amendment rights.

I feel for the student government advisor because while in her position, she may have been required to enforce these unconstitutional policies, but she was also nice to me personally. These administrators are not Antifa, but many of them share the same leftist mentality of winning by any means necessary.

To file our suit, we contacted several legal organizations like the Alliance Defending Freedom (ADF) and the Foundation for Individual Rights in Education (FIRE). We contacted FIRE because they worked closely with Young Americans for Liberty at the national level. After a few months of planning and secrecy, my chapter filed suit. Vinny, my vice president (who later became president) was the sole plaintiff. I was asked to be a co-plaintiff, but chose not to be a party to the complaint out of a concern for my privacy. The lawsuit alleged a number of violations, including the My Little Pony debacle, but the project that grabbed headlines was the petition I organized to condemn the NSA, during which Vinny had been threatened with suspension.

Once we filed our suit, things did not get any better. The administration already did not like us, but now the animosity seemed to come from everyone around us, including professors, the student paper, and even fellow students. The only support we received was from other liberty-minded activists outside of campus.

It was a painful few months, but in the end, we won our case. The school agreed to rescind its unconstitutional policies and pay our legal team $110,000. I wish I had seen some of that money, but the victory was worth a lot more because we fought for the free speech rights of every student on campus. The school's unwillingness to fight the suit was likely because they had been sued for the same type of First Amendment violations a decade earlier.[19]

For a while, there was a sense of freedom around campus, including nonconservative organizations. Yet the lawsuit merely put a halt to certain specific policies; the problem runs deeper than words on paper. The unconstitutional policies we overturned were merely reflections of the anti-free speech sentiment already prevailing across college campuses. Free speech zones are not the problem. They are the result of the Left's anti-free-speech rhetoric. Unfortunately, the leftist hatred of conservative thought is not only chilling free speech, it is also reviving racism.

Not long after Vinny and I left campus, a pro-free-speech student became president of the student government. He was someone who had worked hard to accomplish everything he ever earned, and I had voted for him in a previous election. The school also recognized his achievements and awarded him their most prestigious award. His story should be seen as one of perseverance and determination, but to the Left, it was just another example of white privilege.

Some time after the ceremony, a leftist student government officer blasted the award on Facebook, saying he was "bitter" that the school had chosen to recognize "yet another white cishet [cisgender heterosexual] student who has benefited from male charisma and intimidation." Ironically, the award had been given to students of color the two previous years.

He continued, "I can provide a list of students who actually deserve this recognition, faster than the college can jump to defend why they lack professors of color."

Again, Citrus had multiple professors of color. This student was clearly blinded by a hatred of whites that led him to ignore facts that did not fit his false antiwhite narrative.

Unsurprisingly, he and other leftist bullies attempted to intimidate the student body president when he refused to support their left-wing policies. Later that year, they went so far as to try to impeach him. I made a trip back to my campus the day of the impeachment vote, noting the smug faces of many leftist members. Fortunately, the impeachment effort failed. But ultimately, these attacks are not uncommon. I have helped many students defend themselves against antiwhite racism.

Fighting racism was the reason I originally joined Antifa. But now it is the mainstream left that pushes racist and anti-free-speech rhetoric.

I joined the antifascist movement because I believed they were the best vehicle to fight against racism, no matter where it came from. I eventually left the movement because after talking to many other anarchists, I realized they were hostile not just to fascists, but to anyone with whom they disagreed.

I now regret a lot of my leftist activism. Yet for quite some time, I still remained a leftist. Fortunately, I kept an open mind in college and met some wonderful people who taught me that it is OK to disagree. These people recommended books and online lectures which helped me understand the conservative and libertarian point of view; they are the reason I became a conservative.

I never expected to remain an activist. I thought my grassroots advocacy would end once I was done with school. But when I saw leftist students and administrators promoting bias and hatred against conservatives while violating their rights, I decided to become a conservative activist.

CHAPTER 2

NEVER FORGET WHERE YOU COME FROM: AN IMMIGRANT'S STORY

People often ask how I ended up as an Antifa activist in the first place. The story begins at my impoverished Mexican childhood and my journey to the U.S. as an immigrant. Unfortunately, I drew the wrong lessons from that experience. But it took me a while to figure that out.

I was born in a small town in the State of Mexico called Reyes, La Paz, not far from the nation's capital. My first language is Spanish, and though I have learned other languages, I often still think in my native one. This sometimes gets me in trouble with writing or speaking, as my grammar may be off.

For the first nine years of my life, my family and I alternated between two different homes. My dad's family home was in Chimalhuacán, a dirt-poor city of about seventeen square miles. The city has about a half-million people who live in different barrios. At other times, we stayed at my mom's family home in Nezahualcóyotl, a crime-stricken inner city of about twenty-four square miles. Neither is safe to walk at night, but for many people it is necessary.

My mom tells stories of the Zapatista uprising in the Mexican state of Chiapas that occurred a month before I was born. My parents recall hearing on the radio about how the Mexican government sent military helicopters to fight the insurrection. Allegedly, the Zapatista military arose to fight against inequality in Mexico, specifically in the southernmost regions of the country. I have heard some people incorrectly claim this is the Mexican Antifa. And when I was in the movement, I do recall people being obsessed with them and arguing that we should be more like them. While the movement does belong to radical left-wing politics, and likely would sympathize with Antifa, Zapatista is an independent organization concerned only with Mexican affairs.

Ultimately, Zapista's political influence was inconsequential to the reality that I and other Mexicans lived through. Neither Mexico nor the proposed Zapatista government had the right mentality to lift people from poverty en masse. Instead, people like me and my family were left to endure the tragedies of poverty, corruption, and crime.

When I lived in Chimalhuacán, the house was always full. In total, three different families lived there. Counting my aunts, uncles, and older cousins, the half-constructed concrete home sheltered almost twenty people. Sections of the roof were merely metal sheets loosely fastened on top of one another. In one memory, I recall my mom looking up at a hole in the ceiling and crying as rainwater flooded the kitchen.

One of my first clear memories was the day my aunt died. My mom tells me that days before her death, she simply fell asleep. The doctor said that she was faking illness and could wake up at any moment if she so chose. She never woke up again. She decided to give up on life. I remember people sobbing. This is the first time I remember feeling sadness. Her life and the lives of my cousins were much rougher than mine, even though we lived in the same home.

While my family was poor, my dad worked hard to provide for us. My uncle was nothing like my dad. Although he had four children, my uncle spent all his money on pulque, an ancient Aztec alcoholic drink. He would even sell their furniture to get more money to buy alcohol. My mom often tells me that my aunt's death was the moment she finally realized the desperate poverty we lived in. And it frightened her.

For the time being, we had nowhere else to go. We were still waiting on ancient applications to come to America. Meanwhile, I walked to school on dirt roads because the streets were unpaved. It was especially difficult getting around during storms. The heavy Mexican rains flooded my home multiple times and made it impossible for people to walk around the barrio. I vividly remember one time when I was walking to church with my family. The entire community was forced to march single file along the walls of buildings to avoid getting soaked, while bicycle taxis made a killing driving people across the flooded areas. Even to this day, large portions of the neighborhood are in shambles.

Abandoned cars, broken glass, old tires, and trash littered the streets. People often lit fires to burn their garbage because paying the trashman was too costly, even though we had a dump in the city. One of my sister's friends lived near the dump, and her family had to wear masks to be able to endure the smell. The trashman, of course, was a man driving a wagon pulled by a mule.

On cold mornings, I appreciated the fires because my sister and I used their heat to warm ourselves on our way to school. This practice once made us two minutes late to school, which meant the principal refused our entry.

There was also an incredible problem with stray dogs, which persists to this day. In these neighborhoods, dead or starving dogs are a common sight. I was last there in March 2019. One night, as my wife and I were eating tacos on the street with my family, dozens of dogs ran down the street. My wife decided to feed one of them that was mere skin and bones. Unfortunately, the dog fell in love with her and thought we wanted to adopt him. With tender eyes, it begged for love and began to follow us, only to be attacked by other dogs for trespassing on their territory. The pain and hunger these innocent animals suffer breaks my heart.

My uncle told me about a woman who had been killed by a pack of dogs, which often happens. When my aunt was a little girl in the 1960s, she, too, was attacked by a pack of dogs until my grandpa beat them with a stick. She was on the way to the store to buy candy, and even though she was savaged by the wild animals, she held tight to her two pesos.

In another instance, my cousins, brother, and I were playing soccer on the street when a dog bolted toward us and latched onto my cousin's foot. My brother and cousins hit the dog with sticks and even threw rocks and bricks at it, but it only made the dog bite harder. After the owner forced the dog to let go, my mom came to give my cousin first aid. She then started arguing with the owners, who refused to take responsibility, but all my mom wanted to know was whether the dog was vaccinated. Ultimately, my cousin put his arm around my mom, and they walked a half-mile to the bus stop so they could go to the hospital.

When I was around seven, I saw a puppy across the street and went to pet him. As I was walking back, something latched on to my calf and pulled me to the ground. It was a neighbor's dog who had escaped. I used my other leg to kick its face and was fortunate that he let go of me. I think the only reason I survived was that my dog ran out of our home to defend me. As the two dogs quarreled on the street, I stood, grabbed my leg in pain, and hurried back inside. Yet instead of taking me to the hospital, my mom was forced to heat a large piece of garlic to cauterize my wound. I still remember the excruciating pain. But I also remember being happy to miss school the next day.

Unfortunately, Nezahualcóyotl (Neza for short) is not much better. A common joke is that Neza is the place where dogs would rather stab each other than bite one another. This crime-infested neighborhood has taken the lives of many. Many others live in fear for their livelihood.

Back in the early '90s, while my mom was pregnant with my sister, my grandpa was kidnapped and tortured. He was one of several victims around his neighborhood. They stripped him, doused him with cold water, beat him, and electrocuted him. The sad part is he was snatched from his front door. All the criminals had to do was knock on the door and grab him. The kidnappers let him go several days later after my grandma paid a hefty fine. Although my grandpa was a tough sailor, he had to go to therapy for years to overcome the trauma.

Robberies are much more common. I have never been a victim, but far too many of my relatives have experienced being threatened with a knife or gun. One of my cousins was shot in the leg. Most often, criminals target commuters who are stuck on crowded buses or trains. In these scenarios, criminals stick a knife in someone's back and whisper, "Give me everything you have, and don't follow me when I get off." Even my wife has been robbed in Mexico, and she was only a child. Since she was born in America, she was in disbelief that someone would target children on the streets.

My dad told me he was robbed at least four times. Once, on his way to work at a parking lot near the U.S. Embassy in Mexico City, he was stopped mere minutes after leaving our house in Neza. They took his money and his shoes, so he was forced to come back home. On another occasion, a group of guys came to his work with a gun and demanded all the money in the register. He complied, but a few days later, the strangest thing happened. The head of the gang went to the parking lot, and my dad told him what had occurred. Apparently the gang leader was furious, as that establishment was supposed to be off-limits for some reason. He departed, but came back moments later with a lineup of his street thugs. He asked my dad who had robbed him, and my dad pointed at one. The leader asked my dad if he wanted to take a few shots at him, but my dad simply asked to be left alone. Of course, they did not return any of the money they stole.

One of my fondest memories of my impoverished Mexican childhood is eating Kentucky Fried Chicken for the first time. Even now, I reminisce about the warm biscuits with strawberry jam I ate that night. Any Southerner reading this line will likely laugh, but in my early childhood, eating fast food was so uncommon that it felt like a feast.

Unfortunately, my dad remembers that day differently. He was with my older brother when they went to buy the chicken. My brother must have been only ten or eleven, but that is not a deterrent for criminals, and they were robbed on their way home. The perpetrators took everything he had, but he pleaded to keep the fried chicken so my family had food to eat that night. One of the sweetest memories of my childhood was a day of fear and danger for my dad and older brother.

Even being inside was not entirely safe, as burglaries are also common. I have never met anyone in America who was the victim of burglary. I know the crime occurs, but criminal activity of that caliber is something I have heard about only in news reports, not from almost every one of my neighbors. Both my parents' homes in Chimalhuacán and Neza have been burglarized multiple times, both while we lived there and after we moved to America.

Many Mexicans cement broken glass shards on their roofs and along their walls to protect the home. In my neighborhood, there are no front lawns. The walls typically stand in front of the patio, while the primary living area is tucked in the back, and there are other homes immediately adjacent. The architecture more closely resembles a row of tiny prisons. Of course, as a child, I used to play on these walls by walking on them while keeping my balance.

Even outside of crime, life is a challenge. To take showers, one needs to heat water in a bucket by using two induction cables, which are either connected to a socket or plugged directly into a power generator. If this method sounds dangerous, rest assured, it is. One time, I touched the water while my cousin was warming it for his shower. The electric shock threw me back. Thankfully, I was not injured. Not to mention that there was an outhouse where the toilet was made of cement. To flush it, one needed to use a bucket of water from the home's reservoir. Simple hygiene in Mexico requires more manual labor than most Americans may be accustomed to.

Additionally, I have been injured many times, and not merely because of my natural clumsiness. By the time I was nine, I had pierced my foot with a rusty nail, been bitten by a dog, fell into the home's underground water reservoir, and had a pile of bricks fall on my sister and me. My body is replete with scars from the injuries I suffered as a child. Sometimes I look at them and wonder how I got them. These injuries are a result of the lack of due care for one another by Mexicans.

School was not much better. The Mexican education system is atrocious. In 2012, a Mexican documentary was released, called *¡De Panzazo!,* which loosely translates as *Passed by Luck!*[1] The documentary highlights the country's failed education system and claims that most teachers in Mexico could not pass the exams they administer. The documentary also exposes the system's extreme poverty.

My elementary school lost power because they couldn't afford the electric bill. Instead of paying, they constructed a *gallito*, or small hook, which they attached to an existing powerline. One time, the electric company cut power to my house. In response, my cousin grabbed pliers, climbed an electric pole, and "fixed it" by constructing the same kind of hook as the school. We were ecstatic that we had power again, but this was simply a way to steal electricity from our neighbors.

The picture below shows me in 2018, when I last visited my school. As you can tell, the structure more closely resembles a detention center.

The barbed wire along the walls serves two purposes. The first is to prevent burglaries, which are often committed by the students. The second is to prevent them from ditching class by jumping over the walls. Yet the picture also shows an incredible

My elementary school in Mexico.

improvement from the way I remember the school. At that time, only some inside areas were paved, and the restrooms were tucked in the back of the school grounds because they did not have a working sewer system, and they stank.

To make matters worse, I suffered bullying from my older cousins both in school and at home. In school, the bully was notorious for beating everyone—and this was no mere name-calling or exclusion. I have been punched in the face and beaten in front of my peers and teachers. Unfortunately, my older cousins had previously made my last name notorious in the school. During my first year, after I had been beaten, a teacher asked me for my full name. When I answered, "Nadales," the teacher replied, *"¡Ah! ¡Con razón!"* ("Ah! Now it all makes sense!"). In other words, because of my last name, they refused to believe I was innocent.

I lived through extreme poverty. Yet I am fortunate that my parents did their best to shield us from this tragic reality. My dad is the hardest working person I know. All his life, he has provided for his family, no matter the obstacle. He taught me to be rebellious, passionate, and to fight for a worthy cause. But he also engraved in my mind never to forget where I come from, because when I am lost, my past can point me forward. I do have many happy memories from Mexico, from visiting ancient Aztec ruins, the Mexico City Cathedral, and many natural wonders. Not to mention the fun my brother and sister often shared, like when we used to put empty bottles on the back of our bikes and pretend they were motorcycles. Or the soccer matches we played in the mud and rain.

In the end, our family stayed together, and we persevered. And while my dad likes to remind me that Mexico has a lot to offer, my best memories are in America.

My dad frequently reminds me that we are privileged to have been able to come to this great country. America has its problems, and my dad is certainly not a conservative. Still, like me, he understands that America is one of the most prosperous countries on earth because of the freedoms Americans enjoy. And as my mom says, poverty in America is wealth in Mexico.

Far too many people misunderstand the American dream. Hollywood films and liberal and conservative politicians alike portray it as the achievement of wealth. Some people believe the American dream means to own a house, to have a car, to have a family, to finish college, or land a great job or career. Immigrants typically have this false perception of the American dream because America has a substantially higher standard of living than most of Latin America.

When people define the American dream as wealth, leftist politicians distort it by attacking capitalism and American consumerism. But I eventually learned that the American dream means much more than that. Author James Truslow Adams first coined the phrase the American dream in his book, *The Epic of America*, in which he described it as a dream of a land "in which life should be better and richer and fuller for everyone, with opportunity for each according to ability or achievement."

> It is a difficult dream for the European upper classes to interpret adequately, and too many of us ourselves have grown weary and mistrustful of it. It is not a dream of motor cars and high wages merely, but a dream of social order in which each man and each woman shall be able to attain to the fullest stature of which they are innately capable, and be recognized by others for what they are, regardless of the fortuitous circumstances of birth or position.[2]

The American dream is not about luxury, capitalism, or consumerism. The American dream is about personal self-fulfillment. It is the idea that each of us is free to pursue his or her own path without fearing the shackles of government. Americans are not subjects of the government. We are free individuals who are free to embark on their journey to succeed or to fail. The American dream is not wealth; it is freedom. And it is this freedom that leads to the wealth and prosperity countless Americans enjoy.

This lesson took me years to understand, but it is one I will never forget. To understand where I am going, I must remember where I am from. I come from a place that does not have the freedom and prosperity Americans enjoy. The oppression and corruption of the Mexican government have led its people to poverty, crime, and hunger.

One reason American Antifa is not as extreme as foreign Antifa groups is that America has freedoms that many Latin American, and even some European countries, lack. The blessings of American culture and the American heritage have allowed me to find personal fulfillment. I did not choose to be born in Mexico. As much as I appreciate my heritage, I decided to be an American.

I love America. If I had not come here, I do not know where my life would have ended. However, for much of my adolescence, I hated America.

And the reasons for my hatred are complicated.

* * *

I came to this country when I was nine years old. I remember the drive from the airport to my uncle's house in Azusa. The highway was clear, with little traffic, at least when compared to Mexico City. It was late at night, but the house looked like a mansion. I thought we were rich, even though my family of five was confined to one small bedroom. My dad found a job as a janitor for a laundromat, and we started saving for an apartment of our own, which we were finally able to afford about a year and a half later.

I remember my first morning in America. My mom woke us up early, dressed us, and took us to the Azusa Unified School district to enroll. My mom has always believed in the value of education, and she was not going to let one day in our new country go to waste. As soon as we walked into the district's offices, some administrators made my mom fill out some forms and asked to see our vaccination records. Then my siblings and I took an exam to gauge our understanding of English, which was minimal, at best. We started school that same day, and I enrolled in the final weeks of the second grade.

Adjusting to a new culture was hard enough, but I also experienced a difficult time learning English. I was embarrassed at not being able to communicate with my peers. I was especially ashamed by my thick accent. To give an example, in fourth grade, one of my most worries was the thought of leading the PE class morning stretches. The thought of public speaking is challenging enough on its own, but imagine not knowing essential phrases like, *Bend your knees.*

One morning, I recall walking to school in fear of being called. While I walked, I repeated to myself, "Fold your knees." I incorrectly thought that was the correct phrase because I heard someone say, "Fold the paper."

These little difficulties caused me great anxiety, much more than a child that age should have to bear. But at the same time, the struggle was worthwhile because it helped to strengthen my resolve. My life has been one of continual striving to succeed and to find a way to do the right thing. Due to these struggles, I always look ahead to the next opportunity. I am often in search of the next chance to better my life and those of my loved ones. Thankfully, America gives me that opportunity.

Since I did not speak English well, I often sought out Spanish-language entertainment. Even after I learned English, I still felt more comfortable watching Spanish TV programs. But since cartoons were not readily available in my native tongue, I was left to watch news programming like Univision, *Telemundo*, or Canal 22 for the Los Angeles Area. At the time, TV was just a banal pastime. I did not realize Spanish TV would indoctrinate me into believing an anti-American agenda.

Ironically, by the time I felt comfortable watching English-only programing, mainly my late middle school and high school years,

I stopped watching TV regularly because I saw the attempts by English programs to indoctrinate me. I did not realize the indoctrination had already taken effect.

Many Spanish-speaking networks like to pass themselves off as reliable news sources, but their bias is nakedly apparent. They take advantage of knowing that a lot of their viewers prefer shows in their native language. The coverage among these networks is often uniform in their liberal slant and hatred of American values. According to the Media Research Center, a study conducted from November 1, 2013, to February 28, 2014, revealed Univision and Telemundo's bias. The MRC found that among 667 stories, 45 percent had a liberal slant, while only 6 percent had a conservative viewpoint.[3] In sum, Spanish-language networks are exceedingly left-wing.

But those numbers do not speak to the actual content of the networks. Not all liberal bias is created equal. Their slant goes far beyond journalistic slants everyone comes to expect from the media. Their media strategy for many Spanish-speaking channels is to make Hispanic people feel scared and marginalized. Just like I fell for their lies, they want their viewership to believe they are the only ones that will stick up for Latinos. Unfortunately, Hispanic families invite them into their homes almost daily, and they have an untold impact swaying the political discourse on important issues within Hispanic communities.

I was only in the sixth grade in 2005, when Wisconsin Republican Jim Sensenbrenner introduced the Illegal Immigration Control Act, which sought to criminalize illegal border crossings. It was controversial, and it is one of the first times I remember paying attention to politics. While illegal immigration is obviously illegal, it is not criminal. The penalties are civil, as opposed to criminal sanctions involving jail or prison sentences. This bill would have changed that, and people crossing the border illegally could have ended up in jail.

The contemporary news coverage readily assigned hatred and ill will to the congressman, President Bush, and Republicans in general. From listening to reporters on Univision and Telemundo, I got the sense that this bill was a prelude to internment camps and genocide. The leftist mainstream media seemingly forgot that President Bush's first international trip had been to Mexico, seeking to better the two countries' relationship.[4] As a Mexican immigrant, this made me fear Republicans. And since Republicans are generally more patriotic, this negative attitude eventually morphed into a hatred for America.

To disagree does not mean to hate. But the mainstream media often equate the two because polarizing news increases their viewership and furthers their political agenda. As I learned more about the immigration issue, I became politically involved. During our lunch period in middle school, my classmates and I marched around the school grounds, chanting slogans in support of equal rights while decrying the alleged racism of the Right. In one incident, I suggested to a friend we bring an American flag and stomp on it in protest. He backed off and told me that I was taking it too far. And he was right; I did not know what I was talking about. But then, none of us did. The issue was far more complicated than the media made it out to be. Yet in our minds, the issue was as clear as day and night.

Even before I joined the antifascist movement, I was politically active. For example, I would print flyers against the Iraq War and pass them around my community. But my first significant involvement was at California's Pink Friday protests in 2009.

At the time, Republican Governor of California Arnold Schwarzenegger was attempting to cut down the bloated education budget. Later that year, I attended an Azusa Unified School District meeting, where they were debating whether to cut the arts from high schools. The arts are an important component of education and should not be cut. But local governments had no money to pay for these programs. It is a complicated issue. Nonetheless, both issues were polarized by the Left and boiled down to good versus evil.

According to teacher unions and democratic politicians, the spending cuts were not about California's budget deficit; the move was a personal vendetta by the governor against the less fortunate. As reported by the *LA Times*, Democratic Assembly Speaker Karen Bass "faulted Schwarzenegger for rejecting taxes that Democrats proposed on 'big oil and big tobacco' and instead attacking 'the sick, the young, the elderly, and battered women.'"[5]

The Left often uses emotional manipulation to shame their political opponents instead of engaging in neutral, fact-based policy discussions. The goal is not merely to win the debate, but to destroy the name and reputation of their political opponents. The Left is willing to make any issue personal and leave no survivors to advance their agenda.

After these events, I began to pay more attention to what was happening in America, and wanted to get more involved. I felt passionate about democracy and the idea that we can make a difference if we stick together. Unfortunately, I fell for the empty platitudes that America cared more about waging war than taking care of the homeless and the less privileged. I believed America stood against the rights of people like me, simply because I was not white. I believed the lie that the American dream was dead.

So it is no surprise that when I was in the tenth grade, I refused to stand for the pledge of allegiance. I felt like I was being forced to stand for a country in which I did not believe. Why would I respect a country that had no respect for people like me? That is how my logic went. This act of civil disobedience was momentous for me. It was the first time I went toe-to-toe with someone in authority. Before then, I was merely one of a crowd. I never led any protests or went out of my way to be politically active, besides passing out flyers. I wanted to be a music composer. Yet that changed overnight.

My teacher wanted to punish me for my actions and make an example out of me. She wrote me a referral to the principal's office that was to go on my permanent record. The note was so harsh that the vice principal later told me she had never seen one so severe, even though she routinely dealt with gang-related referrals stemming from fights at school. The school even had to have a uniformed police officer present to combat gang-related violence. On one occasion, a fight left a kid running for his life as a mob chased him across the school grounds. The police officer chased off the attackers. As they walked back to the office, the kid's shirt was covered in blood and he had a gash on his head. Yet she had never seen a referral note like mine.

The punishment was suspension, but I refused to roll over and take it. So I went home and conducted research online and read about the Constitution and the First Amendment. Of course, the irony is not lost on me today that even though I hated America, I wanted to use its laws to defend myself. But unfortunately, this is the way the Left works. The Left is all too willing to ignore the law to silence others, but when they themselves feel threatened, they pretend to care about free speech and civil rights. Whenever I debate students on campus and decry their tactics, they start chanting things like, "What about my free speech?" The Left does not care about free speech. They care about winning by any means necessary. If the argument works for them, they wear it out until they find a better one with which to beat their political opponents.

The next day, I went back to school to speak with my vice principal. I told her I was thinking about suing for having my constitutional rights violated. This was the first time I had ever seen someone in authority react to my words with fear. At first, she said she needed to check-in with the school district. But in less than twenty-four hours, I was allowed back in my class like nothing ever happened. The teacher was forced to swallow her pride and allow me in her class. Sadly, she was likely one of the only teachers brave enough to stand for American values.

Since then, the Left has successfully fought against American values in school. For example, in 2014, a group of California high school students wanted to show their support for America by wearing shirts with the American flag printed on them. The students also faced suspension, but unfortunately for them, the 9th Circuit Court of Appeals defended the school's right to ban the shirts.[6] Just like I fought for my rights, the students should have been allowed to wear these patriotic shirts. But since they stood for America, instead of promoting left-wing causes and revolutionary icons like Che Guevara, the liberal 9th Circuit silenced them.

After my small act of rebellion, I became a celebrity around the school. My peers and other teachers admired me for standing up to "the man," and more impressively, that I won. During passing periods, people would tell me how they wished they had the courage to do the same. As a result, I became emboldened and began searching for more opportunities.

For my senior project, I was tasked to find an advisor and do community service. So I talked to the most radical teacher at school and convinced him to count political activism as community service. It did not take much convincing. Although he was a biology teacher, he likely considered himself an activist first. He was the type who lectured his class about American imperialism, and how Christians were gullible idiots for believing in God. I can still hear him shouting at the top of his lungs, his face red with anger as he railed against Christianity—a lecture that clearly had no place in a human biology class. Radical activism was a public service in his mind.

While in school, I participated in minor protests and acts of disobedience. Every time the U.S. Army came to recruit, I stood next to the servicemen and women to shame them for their service, while decrying the Iraq war. When the student government promoted a boys-versus-girls-themed event, I decried the event as sexist and bigoted. To rail against America counted as community service and helped me earn my high school diploma. Meanwhile, there was no shortage of teachers who encouraged my leftist activism. In contrast, most conservative teachers were afraid to speak out about their beliefs.

In short, the mainstream media, the Spanish-language media, and the ultraliberal education system in California conditioned me to hate America.

They are the reason I joined Antifa.

It has been over a decade since I stopped watching Spanish television regularly. I wish the biased reporting no longer existed, but it makes Spanish networks a lot of money to pit Hispanic communities against mainstream American culture. To this day, Spanish networks continue to push an anti-American message in Hispanic and Latino communities.

Just before the 2018 elections, I was in a Mexican restaurant in Los Angeles, with a TV in the background tuned to Univision. A commercial paid for by Protect Our Kids and Healthcare PAC began playing, at first with an ominous tone. First, we see a black screen as the sound of crying children slowly increases. Then we see a little girl, separated from her family, crying to a uniformed officer, followed by grayscale mugshots of President Trump and other Republicans. The commercial imputes blame to them for a problem that started years before they took office. At the end, the ad urged people to vote for Democrats in 2018. National political strategists understand what works within the Spanish-speaking audiences, which is why they target networks like Univision. Liberals want to play on their viewers' emotions instead of having `substantive debates.

This commercial was, of course, a partisan one—paid for by the democrats. It may sound like a stretch to suggest that the network itself holds the same viewpoint. However, that is not the only commercial I saw that day. The second promoted the nightly news show *Aquí y Ahora* (*Here and Now*), and it began with the same emotional appeal. A commentator spoke about children being separated from their parents at the border, and ended by saying Univision News was the only network standing up to the Trump administration. The implication was that Trump did not care about Hispanics.

An even more striking example of Univision's bias comes from political correspondent Jorge Ramos. Not long after President Trump was elected, Ramos posed with a group of young

Hispanics to send a message to Trump "from the children."[7] When asked by Ramos what message he had for President Trump, the first child replied, "Give a chance to illegal immigrants, and please stop making fun of disabled people." Likely, the only truthful non-rehearsed answer that night came from the child who wanted Trump to outlaw homework. The primary reason for injecting children into political debates is to exploit their youth and innocence. Just as standing against Antifa makes one look like a fascist, disagreeing with the kids' remarks gives you the appearance of not caring about children.

This kind of cynical manipulation is not unique to Spanish-speaking media. Not long ago, singer Linda Ronstadt compared Trump to Hitler and claimed Mexicans were the new Jews.[8] It is sickening that name-calling of that caliber is considered legitimate political commentary. Yet it would be far more dangerous for society to punish her speech.

Personally, I was not a fan of Donald Trump. When I heard that he had announced his candidacy, I could not stop laughing. Like many other conservatives, I thought it was a joke and that he would never become president. I was surprised to see respectable conservatives support him.

The day he was elected, I was mad, and not just because I had lost a five-dollar bet. I thought he would be all-too-willing to drag America back to war, and might even use nuclear weapons. Four years later, he has proved me and other doom-and-gloom critics wrong. While I may not agree with every policy idea he espouses, he has not only kept America out of new wars, but has also taken a special interest in the struggle that thousands of conservative students face on college campuses.

65

In March 2019, I had the privilege of being invited to the White House. After Hayden Williams was attacked at UC Berkeley, the Trump administration made free speech a top priority.[9] It was an honor to be recognized as a free speech activist in this way. But what I found most inspiring were the twelve students who stood behind President Trump, every one of whom had been recommended by the Leadership Institute. President Trump is someone who truly cares about all Americans, no matter their background. The false, reckless, and sensationalized statements by media figures like Ramos, and celebrities like Ronstadt, are not helpful. These people teach minority communities to fear their political opponents and create an either-or mentality that is apt for radicalization.

When I was young, the Left engaged in the same type of yellow journalism against George W. Bush that it uses against President Trump. The defamation Bush received as president follows him to this day as people continue to accuse him of being a war criminal. To the Left, because Bush is a Republican, he must be a diabolical fascist. When President Trump leaves office, he will likely be branded with the same accusations. In contrast, President Obama received the Nobel Peace Prize just for being elected, even though both previous administrations maintained similar foreign-policy strategies.[10]

That same type of rhetoric is what radicalized me into the antifascist movement. If we want to build a better society free of hatred, everyone needs to stop using false and hyperbolic language against politicians of the opposing party. If not, movements like Antifa will only continue to grow.

CHAPTER 3

WHAT IS ANTIFA? A BRIEF HISTORY

Sometime during the Summer of 2011, I was invited by a friend to attend a historical tour hosted by the Black Rose Society. The Society's motto is, *A movement cannot flourish if it is not connected to its roots. So let us bloom!* [1] The group presented a number of these tours throughout the years, mostly sponsored by the Los Angeles Anarchist Black Cross.

The tour included thirteen different stops and twenty specific sites. Interestingly enough, due to building and rezoning, some of the streets presented no longer exist on a map. The tour guide pointed to spots where the International Workers of the World (IWW) offices once stood, and the location of several anarchist riots. Everyone dressed normal; no one was wearing a face covering. However, a few people were carrying anarchist and anarcho-collectivist flags, which prompted the police to follow us for a while. But nothing happened, as the tour was purely educational.

I learned a lot about anarchist history that day. Our guide described various protests of the 1900s, including anarchists chaining themselves to doors, orchestrating riots, and even having gun battles with police. Obviously, the tour was not objective. Every line she spoke made anarchists out to be heroes and martyrs. However, she did say something that rang true: "This is not something you will ever learn in a history book."

Anarchist history, and by extension, Antifa's, is almost nonexistent because history books have been written by the victors. Since American socialists, communists, and anarchists have lost their struggles to the forces of state power time and again, their history is often lost. Meanwhile, the accounts of those who do try to compile this history are often incomplete and conflict with one another. For example, in 2019, when I read Dartmouth Lecturer Mark Bray's book, *Antifa: The Antifascist Handbook*, I found that it shed light on several different radical left-wing groups and movements throughout Europe and Latin America. Yet it was not a complete account. I took issue with him for not writing about a couple of American anarchist movements that I personally know about.

Bray's book brings much of Antifa's forgotten history to the table. He focuses on several antifascist movements from the 1930s to post-World War II. However, just as my tour guide had failed to be objective, Bray fails to impartially characterize the movements. Bray may be an academic scholar and historian, but he is also a radical activist. His leftist bias is present on every page. As such, he sugarcoats the movement as one of heroic revolutionaries who stood ready to oppose tyranny and fascism in all its forms. I sympathize with the idea of helping the defenseless, but Antifa has always been the aggressor, not the defender. Any suggestion that Antifa ever selflessly stood to fend off fascism oversimplifies the case. Antifascist movements during Hitler's time were not concerned with protecting Jews from genocide; they were worried about political power. In some instances, antifascist groups were backed by equally tyrannical regimes.

The Antifaschistische Aktion (Antifascist Action) is the first "Antifa" group in history. Established in the early 1930s, this group was the military wing of the German Communist Party (KPD). Unlike modern Antifa movements, the Antifascist Action was an organization. Modern Antifa groups borrow much of Antifascist Action's imagery and symbolism. The original Antifa logo had two red flags, which were symbols for socialism and communism. Modern Antifa typically has one red and one black flag to symbolize anarcho-collectivism or anarcho-communism. While modern Antifa claims it exists to fight fascism, the original goal of Antifa was to fight for left-wing political power.

Members of the Antifascist Action did not see fascism as an existential threat; they merely saw it as competition. Nazis were not their primary target in Germany, and they often saw Nazism as a lesser evil when compared with other Left-leaning political factions. My theory is that Antifa likely did not target German Nazis because the National Socialist Party was also a self-proclaimed socialist movement. Thus, to some degree, they also opposed capitalism. As Mark Bray writes:

> [T]he socialists and communists were far more preoccupied with each other than they were with the paramilitary formation that would prove to be the most important of them all: the Sturmabteilung (Storm Troops, or SA) of Adolf Hitler's National Socialist German Workers' Party.[2]

In turn, the Antifascist Action and KPD fought capitalists because they were the chief rival of the Soviet Union; both groups were funded and directed by Joseph Stalin.[3] Additionally, the KPD also fought social democrats because the communists believed that anyone who opposed them was inherently pro-capitalist, and thus "objectively" a fascist.[4]

Like modern Antifa, the German Communist Antifa of the 1930s wrongly equated capitalism with fascism. Even at its roots, Antifa was never about fighting an oppressive ideology. Antifa has always been about fighting to destroy capitalism and establish communism. As an antifascist group in Munich declared in 2018, "The fight against fascism is only won when the capitalist system is smashed and a classless society is established."[5] In short, Antifa is fighting capitalism, not fascism. But as any radical communist will tell you, they are the same thing. Fortunately, other governments treat the Antifa movements more seriously than we have in America—at least until recently.

This anti-capitalism movement masquerading as antifascism soon took to the world stage in the late 1930s. According to historian Norman Davies, the rapid rise of Fascism in Italy and Germany worried world leaders. The first to act was Joseph Stalin. He ordered Maxim Litvinov, his foreign commissioner, to join the League of Nations and work to fight against fascism. Thus, the Soviet Union began disseminating the "antifascism" ideology. As Davies writes, "Needless to say, 'anti-Fascism' did not offer a coherent political ideology. In terms of ideas, it was an empty vessel, a mere political dance. It showed its adherents what to oppose, not what to believe in."[6]

Stalin was right. Fascism is a dangerous ideology that should be challenged. But he fought fascism to promote communism, an equally oppressive form of government. Davies continues, "[o]nly in the background was the unspoken dialectic that, if Fascism was to be Bad, the Good had to lie with the originator of anti-Fascism—Joseph Stalin's USSR."[6]

Just as the term antifascism has no real meaning, neither does fascism. This is why in 1944, while Hitler was still chancellor of Germany, George Orwell wrote that fascism had no real meaning, and anyone could use it interchangeably with being a "bully."[7] While fascism once had an underlying philosophy, it has become an insult against anyone in authority. A teenager getting busted for underage drinking would likely call his parents fascists, and no one would think he is misusing the word. Antifa's mission is to fight fascists. But its activists call everyone who is not a radical leftist a fascist. They could call themselves anti-bully and be the same movement. Meanwhile, they would be the real bullies, intimidating people they dislike for no good reason.

This is another important distinction between many radical leftists and Antifa. Anarchists have a guiding ideology that can be traced through history. Columbia professor Dennis Dalton locates the first anarchist debates in ancient Greece, with philosophers like Plato, Sophocles, Zeno, and Carpocrates chiming in.[8] These philosophers rejected anarchism—meaning not sheer unbridled chaos, but the absence of formal leadership. But for them, it was an idea that was worthy of being debated.

Anarchism saw a resurgence as a serious political philosophy in the late nineteenth and early twentieth centuries as a rejection of foreign authority. These ideologies were voiced by organized social movements and by radical individualists who merely wanted to be left alone.

Pierre-Joseph Proudhon is today widely considered the father of anarchism. Proudhon was a French philosopher and a contemporary of economist Frédéric Bastiat; both served in the French

National Assembly. Proudhon introduced some novel theories on "market socialism," which he called mutualism. These were the ideas I was most interested in when I became an anarchist. They rely on privately owned markets, but still adopt the labor theory of value, which finds the value of a product not in the subjective desire to own it, but in the objective effort involved in making it. In the end, Proudhon's was an affirmative ideology. His philosophy was not simply to oppose the free market; he proposed an alternative.

Around the same time, Karl Marx and Friedrich Engels wrote *The Communist Manifesto*. While there is a lot wrong with their theories, at least they proposed a philosophy of how to organize society. In America, other people proposed affirmative theories of anarchism. Emma Goldman defined it as the "philosophy of a new social order based on liberty unrestricted by man-made law; the theory that all forms of government rest on violence, and are therefore wrong and harmful, as well as unnecessary."[9] While some of these movements reserved the option to use violence, they were not reactionary movements, but affirmative philosophies.

Antifa, on the other hand, does not propose any affirmative ideology. Rather, it is a negative reactionary movement. In a void, anarchism would still attempt to organize society. But Antifa cannot exist without "fascists" to oppose. It therefore claims to see fascism everywhere, even where it does not exist.

Ultimately, Antifa is a dumbed-down branch of radical politics. Unfortunately, the weed that is Antifa has infected other legitimate branches of modern radical politics. Although anarchists, socialists, and communists do propose alternative philosophies, Antifa is only about the destruction of those they hate.

This idea explains why not all anarchists are "big-a" Antifa. In 2011, when I was recruiting people to protest neo-Nazis, I came across one activist who was deeply involved in the Los Angeles anarchist movement, focused on immigrant rights. When I proposed we march together at Pomona, he responded that it was foolish to do that. First, he argued that Antifa showing up would only give them more publicity, which they desperately wanted. Second, beating them up would solve nothing. At the time, I did not think much of this argument. But now I see the clear distinction between a real antifascist and an Antifa activist. "Small-a" anarchists typically have a strong ideological framework that they use to oppose fascism. "Big-a" Antifascists care only about beating the daylights out of people without questioning whom they are supposed to oppose.

There is a lot of overlap between radical activists and Antifa, which is why so many radical activists are funneled into black-bloc-style demonstrations. But Antifa is best classified as the military arm of a loose collection of radical activists. It does not stop to think or contemplate alternative philosophies. When one is part of Antifa, it is about action, not discussion.

While Antifa has no direct lineage to the German Communist Party or its Antifascist Action, it still shares the same mission and tactics. It is like modern neo-Nazis who, while not directly responsible for the deaths of millions of Jews in the Holocaust, promote the same hateful and violent ideology. Modern Antifa is simply a wing of communism and radical revolutionary politics— the same philosophies that have murdered millions of people all over the globe.

This truth is not widely known. Thus, taken at face value, Antifa still sounds like a good thing. Yet they use the same tactics as pre-World War II fascists.

That said, not all antifascist groups are created equal. Some groups can be dismissed as terrorist movements, while others walk a fine moral line. Indeed, if there is one story that has the potential to make any conservative or libertarian an Antifa supporter, it is that of the 43 Group's struggle to defend Jewish people in Great Britain immediately after World War II.[10]

As Mark Bray recounts, after the war, there were countless organized attacks against Jews throughout London by self-identified fascist organizations. Like the Nazis, these fascist groups scapegoated innocent Jewish people, and were intent on driving them out of the country. Some of these attacks were heinous, and according to Bray, some Jewish World War II veterans decided they needed to act.

A Judo expert named Morris Beckman, and three fellow Jewish veterans, infiltrated a fascist event and began fighting these fascist supporters. After several scrimmages, they formally organized as 43 Group. For the next several years, their numbers swelled as they attacked a multitude of fascist groups at their events. As Bray portrays the situation, "the attacks took a great toll on British fascists (who no longer publicly identified with the term 'fascist,' given the unpopularity)."[11] Bray implies that the 43 Group is the reason these groups were suppressed.

This story must resonate with any rational person. Just imagine a community under organized attack based solely on its members' religion or ethnicity. Such attacks would surely spark the outrage of decent people everywhere. The story is enough to convince many, especially those within the community, to take up arms to defend the victims. This is the kind of reasoning that inspired me to join the Antifa movement and other anarchist groups almost ten years ago.

However, joining one hateful group to fight another will ultimately backfire. While we should not make perfection the enemy of the good, we should also not pretend that bad is good simply because that option is not the worst. Additionally, Bray downplays different explanations for why fascism never took hold in Great Britain.

First, since the British were part of the Allied military that liberated the concentration camps, being a fascist who targeted Jewish people was unpopular at that time, despite there being fascist elements in Britain both before and after the war. Moreover, Bray presents no evidence to suggest that these isolated elements posed an existential threat to British society. He is thus forced to concede that, "in the grand scheme of British politics such attacks may have been 'fringe activities.'"[12] Bray evidently wants to suggest that the 43 Group stopped another Holocaust. But such a suggestion exaggerates both the threat of such a danger and the 43 Group's importance in British politics.

He is right insofar as real people were being harmed and something needed to be done. People should not stand idly by as innocent people are being hurt. However, the 43 Group organized explicitly in response to imminent attacks. This situation is comparable to the attacks perpetrated against Jewish people in New York City in late 2019.[13] The 43 Group was similar to the Guardian Angels, who announced they would patrol New York streets to protect Jewish people.[14] However, the Guardian Angels are there to protect, not to instigate violence. Force should be used in self-defense only in the face of imminent attack. Bray thus attempts to draw a correlation where there is none. He suggests that the 43 Group is responsible for suppressing the rise of fascism in Britain. But the likelihood of a fascist group rising to prominence in a free Allied country, after that same country fought a war against Fascists, was minimal at best.

The second feature of modern society Bray ignores is the increased efficiency of police combined with society's general desire to prevent and punish hate crimes. Advanced crime-fighting tools allow the authorities to differentiate between nonthreatening individuals and violent racists who pose an imminent threat. American society also has multiple venues through which citizens can peacefully redress their grievances, hold others accountable for their crimes and abuses, and effect positive political change. While one cannot predict the future, privately organized force is currently not warranted in American society.

Bray details many stories and accounts like that of the 43 Group, leading up to 2003. For his purposes, it is not essential to know the complete history of Antifa. It suffices to understand that the modern Antifa groups are typically independent of one another. However, that is Antifa's most significant characteristic.

Antifa is not an organization. It does not hold meetings, nor does it have a formal leadership. While there have been antifascist groups throughout history, Antifa, especially in modern times, is more of a call to action. Thus, Antifa can be seen as an umbrella movement that encompasses other left-wing groups. Just like the label *white supremacist groups* encompasses organizations like the KKK, neo-Nazis, the alt-right and the like, modern Antifa is the banner for many other radical left-wing organizations.

In fact, Antifa is made up of multiple organizations and collectives, such as the Redneck Revolt, the Youth Liberation Front, the Anarchist Black Cross (ABC), as well as local worker unions like the International Workers of the World (IWW). At UC Berkeley, they have BAMN. I have also heard of MEChA (Movimiento

Estudiantil Chicanx de Aztlán) and Students Supporting Justice in Palestine (SJP) being considered part of the movement. These groups rarely call themselves Antifa, although there are some exceptions, such as Rose City Antifa in Portland, Oregon. Still, as far as I can tell, Rose City Antifa is also made up of other local and regional collectives and organizations which operate outside the stereotype of the black mask.

While there is no national Antifa network, there has been a recent push to connect the different chapters who are willing to march under the black flag. Two professors from Purdue and Stanford University created the Campus Antifascist Network (CAN), which aims to connect college antifascist groups.[15] A variety of unions, student governments, college departments, and universities endorse the network and its mission. These endorsements are, in part, why Antifa is growing, as traditional and reputable leftist organizations lend it their credibility.

The most recent national organization to enter the fold is the Young Democratic Socialists of America (YDS), which has over a hundred chapters in over thirty states and the District of Columbia.[16] When I first looked at their website, they listed only about thirty chapters in twenty-five different states. When I began writing this book, there were over eighty chapters. Now, less than a year later, the numbers have swelled to over one hundred thirty chapters on colleges and high schools across the nation. YDS and socialism in general are enjoying a resurgence of public support, and this benefits Antifa, because these groups attract people who are most apt for radicalization.

Since I went public with my story, numerous individuals have talked to me about their experience in radical politics. One person told me she joined YDS at a university in the American

Midwest because she wanted Bernie Sanders to become president. After Bernie lost, she remained friends with other members and became more and more radicalized. Ultimately, she and many in her YDS chapter donned the black mask to protest a variety of events, including a Ben Shapiro speech where someone pulled the fire alarm. She remained active in the movement for well over a year. At first, she enjoyed herself and believed in her cause. However, like me, she developed an independent opinion that conflicted with that of other members. After talking to her compatriots about their disagreements, they grew increasingly intolerant of her. She was isolated, intimidated, and ostracized by her fellow YDS members.

I am by no means saying that these and other left-wing organizations make up modern Antifa. Rather, what I have seen is that these networks help funnel activists to Antifa. I myself never joined an Antifa chapter. I was merely an anarchist who was engaged in animal and earth rights. Yet these chapters and organizations are friendly to the Antifa cause. Thus, when there is a call to action through word of mouth or social media, these groups supply warm bodies who are willing to participate in Antifa's criminal activities.

Another important thing to note is that while Antifa does not have official leadership, it does have thought leaders. I can classify them into three different types: national thought leaders, regional organizers, and independent activists.

Among the national thought leaders are people like Mark Bray, who attained prominence as the author of the Antifa manifesto. He has thereby attained a platform in which he can defend Antifa, and has been invited to many colleges to promote the movement.

Previously, Bray would have been more aptly categorized as a regional leader.

Regional leaders tend to be well-known within their circles of radical politics. Often, they are officers of other left-wing organizations. For example, Dwayne Dixon, who is a professor at UNC-Chapel Hill, is also the leader of his chapter of the Redneck Revolt, a self-identified Antifa organization.[17] The way one becomes a regional leader is simple: just be active for a long time. Many left-wing radicals are only active for a few years. Those who stick around typically take on more responsibility to organize others, and thus gain enough positive reputation to be considered regional leaders.

Independent leaders are those who organize locally. However, it is important not to confuse these types of leaders with independent activists. An independent activist may go to a few protests, but will not lift a finger for the movement on their own. Independent leaders are those who recruit more people and plan smaller protests at the local level. If they are successful, they eventually graduate to regional leadership.

Antifa is not like the military. It's not as if one spends a set number of years in Antifa and gets promoted from private to corporal to sergeant. These leadership roles are the informal way in which radical activists organize themselves. Additionally, every role relies on mutual trust. The only reason Mark Bray was able to write a book on Antifa and interview so many leftist activists was because of the time and effort he put into the movement before he became an academic. But at any point, that trust could be lost and never again reclaimed.

It is also important to highlight the different methods of funding and recruitment for Antifa.

I am frequently asked who funds Antifa. While doing campus tours, I often hear questions such as, "How did George Soros pay you?" or "Is there anyone besides George Soros who paid you?" Countless people hold this belief.

While liberals do spend millions to fund left-wing causes, George Soros did not pay me. No one paid me.

Many people on the Right assume there is a national conspiracy supported by elite liberals who want to instigate violence to suppress conservative thought and votes. My guess is that this belief derives from our sense of self-righteousness. All of us want to believe that our friends and allies are angels who are incapable of harm, and that our opponents are inhuman monsters. Almost everyone perceives themselves to be correct in terms of their own ideology and methods. When confronted with our mistakes, we typically engage in mental gymnastics to justify our system of beliefs. In the process, people find it is easier to blame another than to accept being wrong.

In this context, many conservatives find it easier to think that George Soros hires agitators than to acknowledge that good people can honestly disagree about politics. While Soros may have a lot of political power, he is not the source of every left-wing movement. The idea that Antifa attacks are not funded by anyone is especially scary because it reveals that some people are genuinely motivated to hurt and destroy.

In sum, there is no national Antifa conspiracy. Rather there are multiple localized efforts to disrupt events throughout the country in a classic grassroots manner.

As I explained earlier, all of my activism was self-funded either from personal funds or through the distro I helped run. I cannot speak for everyone, but I never heard or learned of a prominent

national organization that funded anarchist groups. If any significant source of funds existed, it was benefit shows and event fees.
For shows, bands were invited to play at homes or garages where
the cover charge would range from three to ten dollars. When the
show was for a specific cause, the promoters would mention it, but
the cause was never Antifa. The hosts might say that the fees were
going to an activist who had been arrested, a community member
who was in deportation proceedings, or causes such as these.

However, some Antifa groups do have significant sources of
funding. Mark Bray gives half his proceeds to an unnamed group
dedicated to helping Antifa activists.[18] Yet another source of
funding comes from government officials. Late last year, Boston
Antifa members were arrested and charged with assaulting
members of a conservative demonstration.[19] These arrests led
Democratic Congresswomen Alexandria Ocasio-Cortez and
Ayanna Pressley to fundraise to bail them out of jail.[20] Aside from
those sources of funding, I am unaware of any significant organizations or people who fund Antifa activism.

Antifa's history is complicated. Countless stories have not
been well-documented. Thus, much of the history has died
with the activists themselves. While Antifa has technically been
around less than one hundred years, the movement belongs to a
much older communist and socialist tradition. Most, if not all, of
its tactics belong to radical agitators who came before them. This
is why I often find it troubling to hear the lie that Antifa has not
killed anyone.

Firstly, it is not for lack of trying. For example, in 2019, Willem
Van Spronsen, a self-proclaimed antifascist and member of the
Puget Sound John Brown Gun Club (the sister organization to
Redneck Revolt), attempted to bomb an Immigration Control

Enforcement (ICE) office in Washington State.[21] John Brown Clubs and Redneck Revolt groups are Antifa-affiliated organizations that routinely drill and attend protests armed with rifles and tactical gear. Some reports allege that Spronsen threw several incendiary bombs while carrying a rifle at the scene. After ignoring demands by ICE officers to drop the weapon, he was shot and killed. Not long after this incident, there was a drive-by shooting that targeted another immigration office in Texas.[22] While both were unsuccessful, both crimes show an intent to kill by radical activists, or at the very least, a malicious disregard of human life.

More recently, in July 2020, Blake Hampe, who is a "known Antifa member," stabbed Andrew Duncomb in the back with a seven-inch knife.[23] Duncomb's crime was simply filming the violence perpetrated by people like Hampe and other Antifa terrorists.

Indeed, Antifa radicals have killed others throughout history. After the fall of Italy in 1943, Italian antifascist fighters aided Allied countries in fighting occupying German forces.[24] While at first it may appear the antifascists were on the right side of history, their involvement in these battles was mere happenstance. Antifascist forces would have teamed up with anyone to fight the Germans because they craved the power the Nazis held. Once they attained it, so-called antifascists committed hundreds of retribution killings.[25]

Joseph Stalin, who was responsible for funding and promoting the original Antifa organization, is responsible for killing around twenty million people. Other communist revolutions, masquerading as antifascist movements, have killed many others. Che Guevara is seen as a hero by many left-wing radicals for his struggles against the "fascist" American and European powers. When I was in the movement, I saw T-shirts with Che's face on them at almost every social or political event. Countless activists praise him as a model antifascist revolutionary, notwithstanding his own considerable body count.

Likewise, the Red Brigade was an Italian antifascist group active from the 1970s to the mid-1980s, whose founder was inspired by Karl Marx, Mao Zedong, and Che Guevara. This terrorist group also killed numerous people in their striving for power. Additionally, several Spanish Antifa groups operating under the name of the First of October Anti-Fascist Resistance Groups killed eighty-four people between 1975 and 2007.[26]

While I was in Antifa, I heard of antifascist movements in Mexico that had declared war against nanotechnology because they feared it could be used to track and enslave Mexican citizens.[27] A group called Individualidades Tendiendo a lo Salvaje, or Individuals Tending to the Wild, took responsibility for killing a scientist in 2011. They were also responsible for bombing a shipping and receiving facility for the laboratory. I read reports of the attacks in *La Opinion*, a Los Angeles-based Spanish publication, and recognized the players involved. The article details how the attacks severely injured innocent Mexican delivery workers and scientists.

Many Antifa groups possess the extreme mentality required for murder. Yet few of them expressly call themselves Antifa. One must also remember that modern Antifa is made up of many different radical organizations. Antifa often does not kill under the black mask while spray-painting *Antifa was here!* on the walls. Antifa's members kill under their own banner. And throughout history, anarchists, socialists, and communists have murdered millions of innocent people, either in their striving for power, or by creating the same fascist governments they claim to detest.

Antifascist groups are dangerous organizations that are willing to kill for their cause. Unfortunately, the mainstream media wants to glorify Antifa to sell headlines. They are ready to lie and claim Antifa fights only neo-Nazis, the KKK, and other white supremacists, but they are also fighting innocent people throughout the world. In their sights are also people who support capitalism, the free market, and free speech. Although the liberal media may want to push the narrative that no one has been killed by Antifa, it is false. The only people who seem to peddle these falsities are Antifa's mainstream supporters. Even in Mark Bray's book, his introduction states that Antifa is ready to "fight to the death."[28]

Yet American audiences continue to be lied to by mainstream sources which claim Antifa has not killed anyone "in the US in 25 years."[29] While American Antifa has historically been much more tame than its foreign counterparts, the article is a lie.

In late July 2020, Bernell Trammell was shot and killed outside his business in Milwaukee, Wisconsin, where he displayed pro-Trump signs.[30] And in Minneapolis, Minnesota, in the aftermath of the George Floyd riots, police found a dead body inside a destroyed building. That homicide would be classified as a felony murder because the killing was committed during the process of an inherently dangerous felony, which in this case was the wanton and willful arson and destruction of property committed by Black Lives Matters rioters.

On the back of *Antifa: The Antifascist Handbook*, Bray quotes an antifascist activist, "Murray from Baltimore." Murray says:

> You fight them by writing letters and making phone calls so you don't have to fight them with fists. You fight them with fists so you don't have to fight them with knives. You fight

them with knives so you don't have to fight them with guns. You fight them with guns so you don't have to fight them with tanks.[31]

Murray's statement accurately reflects the way Antifa members think. When I was in Antifa, radical activists were mostly in the primary stage, fighting fascists with protests and letters. After realizing their tactics were failing, Antifa radicals are escalating their "activism" to stage two: physical attacks. This is exactly what we are seeing on American streets today. The Antifa demonstrations are not peaceful protests, but violent riots and occupations of American territory, like Seattle's infamous CHAZ. Amid the civil unrest unleashed by the killing of George Floyd, Americans are beginning to see what Antifa is capable of, including assaults, arson, rioting, and murder. As long as mainstream liberal figures continue to support Antifa, the violence will only get worse. Eventually, Antifa radicals will begin to arm themselves to engage in gun scrimmages with police like radical activists did in the early 1900s, in Los Angeles.[32]

More troubling still is that Bray suggests Antifa action should not be limited to opposing the Far Right, but should also fight what he refers to as everyday fascism.[33] According to Bray, force is needed to "increase the social cost of oppressive behavior to such a point that those who promote it see no option but for their views to recede into hiding." This can include tactics like protests, doxing, disruptions, and riots.

I have met those whom Bray calls "everyday fascists." Bray portrays them as the scum of the earth: people who, while not outwardly Nazis, supposedly promote "oppressive" politics. These people are often just students around eighteen to twenty-two years old, and sometimes younger. These are the students I help every day as a free speech activist. If Antifa activists and other anarchists genuinely believe in the purity of their cause, they should attempt to persuade and convince their young peers, not intimidate and hurt them.

How is it "oppressive" to carry a sign that reads, "Hate Crime Hoaxes Hurt Real Victims"? How is it oppressive to wave an American flag and ask, "Do you love America?" How is it oppressive to invite an economist to campus to talk about business and capitalism? How is it oppressive to ask these questions?

For Antifa, there is no such thing as freedom of speech. They reject this basic tenet of American society. As Bray says, "At the heart of the Antifascist outlook is a rejection of the classical liberal phrase…that I disapprove of what you say, but I will defend to the death your right to say it."[34] Yet the media pretends they are somehow the "good guys."

Antifa is not fighting imminent threats of danger, and it never has. Modern Antifa is attacking students for mere political disagreements. If these activists are not stopped, they will escalate their violence to all-out warfare, as Antifa groups have done in the past.

CHAPTER 4

ANTIFA'S TACTICS: A BASIC GUIDE

I have been an activist for over ten years, and for the last seven I have been a conservative. During that time, I have seen Antifa rise from an obscure fringe group to mainstream prominence. I am not the ultimate authority on this subject, but what I can uniquely offer is perspective from both sides. The following is a simple guide to understanding how to combat some primary tactics Antifa uses to intimidate and silence conservatives.

As I argued earlier, Antifa is simply a branch of radical politics. Thus, Antifa activists, like other anarchists, socialists, and communists, subscribe to the old creed that the ends justify the means. This is a dangerous doctrine that may be used to justify any atrocity so long as the ends are deemed worthwhile. For the Left, the end has always been defined as a state of absolute material equality. But as shown by countless radical left-wing movements throughout history, that promise remains unfulfilled.

Antifa in action is often described as a mob. But while there are some similarities, this description falls short in several respects. As I mentioned earlier, I never intended to harm another person when I was in Antifa, and thankfully I never did. However, being part of the group meant accepting the possibility of physical conflict. Thus, the mob mentality begins to creep to the surface. That said, people in a mob act spontaneously and often simply fall into unplanned violence, while Antifa actively seeks it and their attacks are often premeditated.

Direct Action

First, it may be helpful to explain what the term "direct action" means. Some people may think of it as a tactic in its own right, but direct action is the umbrella under which most, if not all, of Antifa's tactics fall. Direct action means to take matters into one's own hands to enact political change. It is vigilante "justice." Antifa does not wait for the system to act; it goes out and does it. Antifa will always pretend that its violent actions are taken in self-defense. It is the duty of conservatives to expose this lie by any legal means.

The Black Bloc

The black bloc is not a separate entity, as some may think, but a military-style tactic wherein dozens, sometimes hundreds, of left-wing activists march in unison, concealing their identity with masks and black clothing. Many people believe black bloc is Antifa because black bloc demonstrators often engage in political violence. However, the black bloc is just one of Antifa's many faces. There are many Antifa activists who never participate in these types of protests, but are nevertheless deeply involved in the Antifascist movement.

The black bloc is a relatively new tactic that falls under the umbrella of direct action. It started in the 1970s in West Germany, and was routinely used by squatters to avoid police detection.[1] When marching in a group, the black bloc camouflages the identity of criminal activists. However, many left-wing radicals fail to perform this tactic correctly, which gives conservatives the opportunity to defend themselves.

For this tactic to be effective, every piece of clothing has to be common, and it has to be black. I have seen some activists wear red bandanas, black leather jackets, motorcycle helmets, blue jeans, boots, or other attractive pieces of clothing during marches. The purpose of the black bloc is to avoid identification. Wearing distinctive or provocative clothes defeats this purpose. I remember seeing activists wear punk outfits, including spiking their colored hair and sporting bright-colored vests. Somehow they thought that covering their faces with red bandanas would preserve their anonymity.

For the protection of everyone in the black bloc, everyone one must wear generic clothing. One mistake that undercover officers have made is to wear their police-issued boots. Any seasoned antifascist activist will easily spot them in a crowd. When I attended marches, I wore cheap black shoes that I would throw away after two weeks. I also wore black jeans or chino-style pants, black winter gloves I bought at the dollar store, a black beanie, and a zipper hoodie that was one size too big. Nothing I wore had a logo or any unique characteristic. The "black mask" was merely a generic black bandanna, which I also bought at a dollar store. All these articles of clothing helped me blend in with my fellow activists.

Underneath my hoodie, I had a backpack in which I carried a change of clothes for when I left the scene. The concealed backpack should be recognizable, but not exceptionally so. Hiding the backpack during the protest serves as a red herring to police because the bag will not show in any photos, nor will anyone remember seeing it. When I marched in the black bloc, I waited until a protest had ended so I could run to a secluded area to put my hoodie in the backpack and change. Since no one remembered seeing my backpack, I felt comfortable walking away as if I was oblivious to the rally.

When done effectively, the black bloc is a powerful tool for avoiding arrest. At one protest, for example, a former friend of mine was getting arrested by a sole officer. Meanwhile, two other anarchists saw the altercation and rushed to help. One pushed the officer, while the second punched him in the face. As the cop was rocked back, they helped my friend run back into the black bloc to avoid detection. If the activists were wearing recognizable clothing, they would all have been targeted for arrest later.

The best way to combat the black bloc is obvious—look for identifying characteristics.

At a 2018 rally, an Antifa activist used the black bloc to attack a conservative by hitting him over the head with a bike lock.[2] The perpetrator was Eric Clanton, a professor of philosophy at Diablo Valley College in Northern California. The bike lock cracked open the student's head, which caused him to bleed as he suffered a concussion. Fortunately, Clanton made several mistakes that led to his arrest. First, he was not wearing a beanie, so his hair was partially exposed. Second, he wore his sleeves rolled back, so his white skin color was apparent. Third, he wore a backpack on the outside. Thus, while his face was covered, he did not remain anonymous. Numerous videos and pictures of the protests lead to his identification.[3] Unfortunately, Clanton reached a plea deal and was sentenced to a mere three years of probation, even though he originally faced several years in prison.[4]

The black bloc is a powerful tactic to avoid detection. However, there are a lot of activists who do not know how to perform it correctly. Their failure is useful to conservatives because taking photos and videos of these activists can lead to their identification and arrests. Pierce the black bloc by identifying and holding individual activists accountable for their criminal behavior.

Propagande Par le Fait

Propagande par le fait, or propaganda by the deed, is a form of direct action that encourages violence.

I first heard about propaganda by the deed from a song by the band A//Political, the title of which is "Propaganda by Deed."[5] The lyrics describe preparing to commit an act of violence. However, there is more than merely the voluntary act of violence. The propaganda aspect is a critical component in the formula. Antifa does not only want to attack people. Antifa wants to send a message with each strike so its criminal acts intimidate its victims and become an inspiration to others. The mentality is simple: *If I can get away with attacking someone, then you can too!*

The best way to combat this tactic is to hold perpetrators accountable and then publicize their failures. As I mentioned in the introduction, Hayden and I were once physically attacked at the UCLA. The event we were attending was hosted by the local Turning Point USA chapter, and dealt with fake news and civility in politics. One of the speakers then brought up the Covington students and the media's botched coverage, when he was interrupted by an audience member. This kid then slammed his palms on the desk and yelled, "Black trans lives matter! You're all fascists!"[6] No one was talking about African American issues or trans lives, but he felt it necessary to interject at that moment.

The event was on the top floor of a building with an outside balcony-hallway. It was around 7:00 p.m., and already dark. I was on the balcony, looking in through a window, with Hayden at my side. I did this because every seat was taken at the event. When the kid first walked in, Hayden thought his demeanor intimated that he might cause some trouble. He seemed moody, not smiling or talking to anyone. He walked toward the back row of the classroom. We stopped paying attention to him after a while because he seemed to be engaged in the event. But that changed quickly.

When the disruption occurred, I pulled out my phone to record it. My camera took a few seconds to open, so I did not capture everything. However, on his way out, the kid slapped someone's phone away and pushed out the door. As the student walked out, he saw me trying to record. He was walking away from where I stood, but then took a couple of steps toward me and hammer-punched me twice. I lifted my arms so the punches landed on my forearm. As he walked away, he banged his head on a metal window awning. That is when my phone began to record.

Never before had someone attacked me without provocation. Hayden and I followed him while I dialed the police. Unfortunately, we were unaware that a second guy was throwing stink bombs inside the room. While we were going down the stairs, he also began to threaten us.

"Let's find a dark corner, and we'll settle this," he kept yelling.

My first instinct was to take off my backpack and wear it in front in a defensive manner in case he was waiting for us at the bottom of the stairs. But at that point, their intent was to avoid us.

When it became apparent that we would not abandon our pursuit, his tactics became offensive. He would run around pillars and hallways so he could rush behind us and assault us. Numerous times, Hayden and I were forced to jump out of the way to avoid a blow. Eventually, he confronted us at a quad near the science building. He and Hayden began exchanging insults, but then the second guy approached, puffed up his chest, and then squared up. He started throwing punches, and landed a couple to the side of Hayden's head. I remember yelling at the police dispatcher on the phone, describing what was happening, but when Hayden fell to the ground, I ran toward them and pushed the other student off him. It felt weird to push him. My arms were weak, but I pushed him far back. The feeling was likely my adrenaline kicking in.

As I helped Hayden up off the floor, the other kid stood and ran away. I took a second to make sure Hayden was OK. He was rocked, but none of the punches landed to his face. We looked around for both perpetrators, but saw only the first guy. He was struggling to run away—he was carrying a big backpack and was wearing big boots.

The pursuit led us to a main street in front of UCLA, where we saw a several police cars, who were likely responding to my call. We flagged down an officer, and she jumped out of her car and sprinted toward the suspect. The next thing I saw was him struggling with her. It did not take much for her to get the cuffs on him. A bystander began to record the arrest, and the dispatcher told me to wait nearby so an officer could question me.

I looked at the kid, who now sat on the curb, restrained, with his hands behind his back.

He yelled, "Why aren't they in handcuffs? They're the fascists!"

This statement is evidence of the Left's state of mind. They can attack someone without provocation, but still feel like the victim.

The officers questioned Hayden and me separately, and took pictures of my bruised arms for evidence.

The officer asked me, "Do you want to go press charges?"

I said yes, so an officer took me to his car so he could drive me to the station nearby. Before we left, he made me wait inside for a few minutes before we took off, which gave me time to reflect. That's when I began to struggle with my decision to press charges. After I arrived at the station and was taken to an interrogation room, I began to have flashbacks to when I was arrested several years prior. I had made the stupid mistake of questioning an officer during a lawful stop, which ended up putting me behind bars for thirty-six hours. Being arrested was a terrifying moment, and I do not wish it upon anyone.

Yet when the officer walked in with the official complaint form, I signed my name on the dotted line. I knew that if we allow people to get away with minor nuisances, we are only paving the way for much more serious criminal behavior.

After I left the UCLA police station, I called my wife to tell her what happened. Then I walked back to the event. Apparently, after we left, a third person began disrupting the event and was escorted out by officers. That made me chuckle. But at least no one else was hurt.

Hayden and I then helped the students take supplies to their car, and went to find a hotel to spend the night. After we finished checking in, we went to our favorite taco truck in Inglewood, near LAX. We ordered our food and pulled up some milk crates to sit in the open air.

Nevertheless, as Hayden and I were eating and joking around, like friends do, the thought hit me. That kid was in jail. He would probably be released soon after being booked, but for now he was likely sitting in a jail cell, waiting to be processed, while Hayden and I were having a good time. Yet it occurred to me that if I had not pressed charges, he would likely be doing the same thing—joking around with his friend who attacked Hayden, and bragging about their exploits. Both would have been emboldened by getting away with assaulting two conservatives and disrupting an event.

Propaganda by the deed often takes the form of minor incidents like this. The student's actions would have inspired others to disrupt the next event, and the next, until things escalated to riots, as they have at UC Berkeley.[7]

Propaganda by the deed is why violence spread like wildfire amid the George Floyd protests. Antifa orchestrated riots in radical strongholds like Portland and Minneapolis, which allowed other radical groups to follow suit. Not long after, the violence became the propaganda as Antifa supporters falsely argued that this kind of wanton destruction was itself a form of speech—the "language of the oppressed." Had liberal politicians allowed law enforcement to take a more active approach in deterring Antifa violence, the riots would been limited to the few original agitators. However, since many liberal politicians refused to condemn the violence, Antifa activists and other rioters felt they could get away with burning their cities to the ground.

When I began writing this book, modern Antifa was in the first stages of its radical tactics. But the more riots Antifa orchestrates, the more success it sees as liberal politicians refuse to actively combat, denounce, or even acknowledge its criminal activity. And Antifa is not finished. It is more than willing to escalate the riots, because its tactics are not performed in a vacuum. These criminal acts are part of a larger plan to shut down conservative thought and speech altogether. Therefore, it is up to every conservative activist to hold Antifa accountable for its criminal behavior.

When Antifa activists fail, publicize it. Because when its failure is broadcast, Antifa begins to lose support. These attacks were once rare, but unfortunately they are becoming more and more common, and they are being perpetrated against innocent people.

What was my crime in the story? Attending a conservative event? Recording a criminal act? According to Antifa, it was me being a fascist.

A few months later, Hayden and I went to court for the first appearance. We arrived early and sat in the back, waiting to speak with the prosecutor. Finally, the kid walked in with his mom. This was especially painful for me because I remembered my mom's anguish when I was in jail. His mom had the same worried eyes my mom did. But then I spoke to the prosecutor. After I walked him through the events as I remembered them, he told me his purpose in this role was simply to deter minor criminal acts, with the hope that the perpetrators would not commit them again. He further emphasized that the legal system is the best way to peacefully resolve such disputes, because otherwise, senseless vigilante violence would rule the day. While it was a tough decision to press charges, I am glad I did. I do not want to live in Antifa's world, where its activists can attack innocent people without repercussions.

I do not like being assaulted. I do not like going on campus and having to look over my shoulder, thinking that at any moment, someone may attack me. Unfortunately, I have been involved in other altercations on campus since that incident, and I know of others who have been severely injured by the activist left. These incidents often do not get the attention they deserve. But that is the risk I chose to take to defend student rights and their free speech.

"Peaceful" Propaganda

Banner drops and zines are antifascist tactics to spread propaganda and misinformation for the antifascist cause. I put the word *peaceful* in quotation marks because at first glance, they appear to be a legitimate exercise of the activists' First Amendment rights. However, just like every other Antifa tactic, this practice is often backed with the threat of violence, and in some cases, the type of speech involves other criminal behavior.

Banner drops involve creating a large banner with a radical message that is then "published" in a public space, like on top of a building, parking structure, or freeway overpass. I have conducted multiple banner drops throughout Southern California.

This tactic is not exclusive to Antifa. Driving down the I-10 freeway around Los Angeles, one will often see small-a banners that read, *NO ICE*, tied to the fence on an overpass. Yet while these banner drops appear to be innocuous, there are two reasons this type of activism is often unlawful. First, banner drops often involve breaking and entering into privately owned buildings. Breaking into places like this can often involve the use of force. Second, when a banner is hung off a freeway overpass, there is a risk of it falling onto oncoming cars and creating an accident.

The second tactic involves creating flyers, posters, pamphlets, or zines, which I distributed for free. While I was an anarchist, I routinely engaged in this practice. I must have printed two dozen pamphlets and newsletters, using old printers I found in the garbage. While I often simply printed theories on government oppression, many other antifascist activists perform the tactic in an unlawful manner, which would not be protected by the First Amendment.

First, some antifascist activists disseminate their literature with the use of force. Second, modern activists frequently dox private individuals. Doxing requires a more complete explanation, which I will provide below. So for now, I will focus on the unlawful use of force while distributing flyers.

At UC Davis, I have helped several different student organizations, including a pro-life group that was being bullied by the administration and leftist students. Every time I have advised a conservative club at this university, we are accosted by student activists, sometimes more than once a day.

Here is how the scenario typically plays out: Early morning, I arrive with the students to inflate a free speech ball, which is a twelve-foot beach ball on which we encourage people to write messages supportive of free speech. Once the ball fully inflates, we roll it to an area with heavy foot traffic. But we are sure to stand clear of any alleyways so people who do not want to talk to us can avoid us.

This typically goes well for about a half-hour, but then leftist students begin to arrive. Sometimes they are outright confrontational. There have been multiple incidents, at UC Davis and several other schools across the country, in which a leftist student used a knife to stab the ball, and then ran away. Specific to UC Davis, sometimes the leftist students pretend to merely be interested in providing an alternative to our speech. That in itself is fine. However, their "speech" typically involves them interrupting our conversations with other people. They attempt to lure these interested students away from our group, or block them by standing between them and us. When I call out their behavior, they yell back, "What about my free speech?"

There are two reasons why this type of speech is not protected by the First Amendment. The first is that the First Amendment covers more than just speech. There are several protections enshrined in the First Amendment. The first is freedom of religion, then free speech, and then the free press. After that is freedom of assembly, and lastly, the freedom to peacefully redress grievances. In total, the First Amendment expressly protects five different rights. Often, these rights compete and clash with one another.

In this story, the specific right at issue is the freedom of assembly. Although it is not spelled-out in the First Amendment, the Supreme Court has extended the right of assembly to the right of freedom of association.[8] In a nutshell, freedom of association is the freedom to join groups and not to be forced into joining one. This right also protects people from outside disruptions that make it hard to peacefully assemble, as well as the right to refuse membership to certain people. Thus, while free speech is extremely important, it is not the only right at stake in the First Amendment, and it is not always the paramount value in all situations.

The UC Davis radical activist disrupted the students' freedom of association by inserting himself into a conversation to which he was not privy. At first, it was an indiscretion that merely warranted a verbal warning. But after repeatedly being told to stop, he continued his attempts to coerce students, who were interested in joining the conservative club, into taking his literature. If they refused, he would annoy them until they walked away. Thus, while he cried foul and demanded his freedom of speech, this right may sometimes be curtailed to allow for freedom of association. In this case, that is exactly what happened. The conservative students were forced to call campus security and tell them what was happening. When the police arrived, they instructed the activist student to stay at a comfortable distance from the conservative students so as not to disrupt their peaceful activities.

However, there is another way his speech was not protected. In *Chaplinsky v. New Hampshire* (1942), the Supreme Court established the fighting words doctrine.[9] Fighting words are defined as "those which, by their very utterance, inflict injury or tend to incite an immediate breach of the peace." In this case, a preacher had been arrested while decrying a public official as a "God damned racketeer" and a "damned fascist."[10] It is important to note that the doctrine has been questioned by other rulings, since the words by the plaintiff in *Chaplinsky* were directed at a public official. However, the case controls this interaction. As mentioned earlier, the radical activist was yelling in my face, and he became belligerent when we asked him to leave us alone. Such interaction had the potential of creating an immediate breach of peace if not controlled by a neutral third party such as an officer of the peace.

However, while both these tactics appear at first glance to be based on a peaceful free speech foundation, they are not. Recall the Antifa activist named Murray from Baltimore, who claimed that Antifa fights with letters so it does not have to fight with fists, knives, and ultimately tanks. Some might say Murray's words are merely a form of anticipatory self-defense, and demonstrate a desire for a situation not to escalate toward violence. However, from personal experience, I know this to be false.

It is one thing to defend with force. It is another thing to threaten force if a situation does not play out favorably for your cause. The radical Left often does the latter. Antifa is not saying, *If you attack us, we will fight back*. Antifa is truly saying, *If you don't shut up, we will attack you*. The first would be a permissible conditional threat, but the latter is an unlawful threat against peaceful individuals. If they fail to convince people, or if they fail to thwart someone else's right to free speech, force is always an option to Antifa's members.

The answer to hateful speech is more speech, not violence and intimidation. The tactics of physical confrontation will be covered below, but the way to fight against "peaceful" propaganda is to have true peaceful speech. That is how conservatives are fighting back against this particular tactic.

Every time conservatives host a recruitment table, or libertarians sponsor an event on campus, we take the fight to the Left by challenging their liberal hegemony. Due to the effort of countless student activists across the nation, the conservative movement is challenging unconstitutional campus policies that are used to silence conservative thought. But more importantly, they are changing these colleges' extreme culture. A majority of students are not liberal because they believe the Left is superior; many are liberal because they have never been exposed to conservative thought. That is the reason Antifa has to resort to violence. Because if conservatives are allowed to speak freely, they will peacefully convert more of Antifa's base toward liberty-oriented politics.

"Subvert"

Even though I am now a conservative activist, I still listen to the music of my teens. The type of music I listened to varies in style, but most of it is political. One of my favorite bands is the Zounds, which I think most people would find catchy, as the musicians were once jazz musicians, turned punk. They are probably the most talented punk group from their generation. I also had the opportunity to meet and talk to their front man, Steve Lake, around the time the UK was experiencing a resurgence of anarchist direct action. Zounds once wrote a song called "Subvert," which exemplifies a growing tactic by leftist professionals, particularly professors. The song mentions working as an agent for revolution in your workplace.

In this context, to "subvert" means to undermine someone's authority, or disrupt the workplace for revolutionary purposes. In the case of Antifa-supporting professors, it means to use their position and authority over students to shut down conservative and libertarian speech in academia. This tactic is routinely practiced by leftist faculty. The mission of a college or university is to teach students useful skills for their professional careers, and above all, teach them how to think. Many leftist professors subvert their college's mission by terrorizing conservative students and teaching everyone what to think. This tactic is the antithesis of liberal education. Thus, professors who undermine the true mission of a college should be fired and never again allowed to hold a job in academia.

I have received some pushback on this stance from civil libertarians who believe I am fighting against the free speech of professors. To be clear, I do not think people should be fired merely for having radical political beliefs. When a professor at Fresno State University tweeted her disdain and hatred toward Barbara Bush after her death, many people in the conservative world were calling for to be fired.[11] Yet she was not teaching at the time, and she made the comments on a private platform unrelated to the school. Therefore, I do not believe she should be fired. However, I do believe that if a professor's political bias hinders her ability to faithfully fulfill her proper role, then that professor should be dismissed.

Say, for example, that I decide to take a job in an Apple Store. Let us further assume that I personally believe Samsung phones are superior to any Apple product. My mission as an employee of the Apple Store is to sell Apple products. Regardless, I should not be fired for thinking Samsung phones are better. Moreover, so long as I do not have a contractual obligation that prohibits me from criticizing Apple on my private platform, I should be able to speak freely. However, if every time a customer enters the store, I encourage them to walk around the corner and buy a Samsung phone instead, Apple would have just-cause to fire me. Similarly, liberal professors should be fired for their speech only when they act on a personal bias that hinders the education of their students.

I first encountered this question when Jeff Klinzman, an English professor at Kirkwood Community College in Iowa, was allegedly fired for claiming he was part of Antifa. At the time, I believed that speech should be punished only if it creates an imminent threat of harm. However, after some digging into the issue, I realized I was applying the wrong standard in this case. As a professor at a public college, Klinzman was a public employee of a government agency. Thus, when judging a government agent's speech, the Supreme Court case *Connick v. Myers* (1983) controls.[12] According to Belmont University assistant law professor David Hudson Jr., "If the speech touches on matters of public concern, then the court balances the employee's right to free speech against the employer's interests in an efficient, disruption-free work-place."[13] In other words, the speech of public employees is held to a higher standard than that of a private citizen.

Antifa is, of course, a matter of public concern in contemporary American politics. Thus, a court must balance the professor's speech with the mission of the university not to create an inefficient and disruptive workplace. It is one thing for a professor to be sympathetic toward Antifa's cause, but another to claim to be part of Antifa, as Klinzman did. This is because Antifa has no lawful or legitimate aims. Antifa's only aim is to silence debate and opposition, by any means necessary. A professor who claims to be part of Antifa is therefore acknowledging his intention to engage in these kinds of tactics. In this case, then, the college was right to terminate the professor. Left-wing educators may have a constitutional right to talk about politics, but they do not have a constitutional right to be professors.

Subversion of this kind is one of the most prevalent tactics used by leftist educators. I have personally dealt with professors who mock conservative students in the classroom, turning from philosophical objections to ad hominem attacks on non-liberal ideologies and students, which create a hostile learning environment. However, it is also easy to fight. Thanks to modern technology, cell phones are the key to fighting back against biased professors. When leftist professors abuse their platform and position to indoctrinate students or shut down opposing ideological views, conservative students have a duty to expose their bias to the administration or to friendly media outlets if the university refuses to act, as often happens. If I had recorded my biology teacher preaching against God instead of teaching about mitosis, he would rightly have been fired.

In 2017, a student at Orange Coast College in California caught one of his professors proclaiming that Donald Trump's election was an "act of terrorism."[14] The video was posted online and spread like wildfire. Unfortunately for the student, he was suspended for that recording, and a fight ensued to get the school to back down. Multiple activists from different organizations advocated for the student's free speech rights. Even the local publication, the *Orange County Register*, chimed in with an editorial that read: "Recall board if OCC student isn't reinstated."[15] Thanks to this massive campaign, the student's suspension was rescinded a few weeks later.

While I enjoy the outcome of that story, I want to caution anyone who plans to do this type of activism. Many states have wiretapping laws, otherwise known as two-party consent statutes. These laws prevent people from being recorded without their consent if they have a reasonable expectation of privacy. If you plan to do this type of activism, check the laws in your state.[16] In some states, the recording will not be admissible in court. Other statutes may apply legal penalties. And in some places, professors may go on the offensive, and others may not be so willing to back down.

For example, at Syracuse University, one of Campus Reform's student correspondents, Justine Murray, has been routinely exposing the school's liberal bias and abuse against conservatives. This has led several liberal professors to target and harass her online.[17] In one incident, according to her, a professor followed her in the dark, pulled her, and began to berate her for being a conservative. Although she filed a complaint, the school has been dragging their feet on the issue.

Another example comes from Weber State University, where philosophy student Michael Moreno recorded one of his professor's antiwhite racist lectures. As the recording shows, the professor believed that outer space did not exist and was merely a "projection of white fantasies." The recording goes on to expose many other antiwhite comments by the professor.[18] Unfortunately, Michael was placed under investigation by the school for making the recordings public.[19] While the video went viral on YouTube, I was unaware of it for months. When I learned about the video, I searched for Michael and messaged him about it. He told me that the investigation had concluded, and I was too late. The administration had placed him on academic probation for exposing his racist professor.

I strongly believe that if Michael had had proper legal representation, he would not have lost his appeals. Nevertheless, I tell this story to warn would-be undercover journalists that activism is not a joke. There are serious legal issues that one must consider when trying to expose nefarious conduct by the Left.

In a more extreme scenario, pro-life activist David Daleiden is facing several felony charges in California for secretly recording doctors from abortion clinics, in which they admitted selling fetal body parts.[20] So before you consider engaging in this kind of activity, be smart and check the laws in your state.

Deplatforming

As previously discussed, deplatforming is the act of denying or depriving a speaker of his or her ability to exercise free speech. This tactic can take many forms, including pressure on the venue, systematic shunning and marginalization, or even physical force.

One way to deplatform a speaker is to keep people from attending their event. This can be accomplished by taking up seats or buying up tickets to prevent conservatives from reaching their audience. In November 2017, Robert Spencer (not to be confused with the white nationalist Richard Spencer) spoke to what appeared to be a sold-out room. However, shortly into his speech, almost every student walked out.[21] This tactic disrupted the event, but the worst part was that supporters waiting outside to be let in were not allowed to enter. This planned disruption forced the students to cancel the event.

To prevent a situation like this, one must prepare well in advance of an event. Before every conservative gathering, especially controversial or highly publicized speaking engagements, students should monitor Facebook, Twitter, Snapchat, and Instagram to find out what to expect. For example, when conservative commentator Michael Knowles spoke in Missouri, the Young Americans for Freedom group hosting him performed beautifully.[22] Before the event, a student preempted a planned walkout by exposing it to the audience. All he had to do was walk toward the podium and read the message he found on Snapchat. Such a tactic preemptively reverses the roles of the protesters. People no longer saw the strike as a disruption, but as an immature tantrum by childish students who could not bear to hear another point of view.

Unfortunately for Knowles, he was also assaulted that night with a water gun. It may seem absurd to think of such an act as assault, but one must remember one thing: Antifa and its supporters are always willing to escalate. This is what happened after British politician Nigel Farage was assaulted with a milkshake.[23] At first, it was called an act of nonviolent resistance. However, that type of attack escalated to throwing milkshakes at Andy Ngo while several Antifa agitators beat him.[24] If Portland Mayor Ted Wheeler had taken this crime seriously and invested police resources into getting justice for Andy, the city and its residents would not have been under siege for over two months following George Floyd's death.

It is also essential to befriend campus police and let them know of the potential disruption. At many of my own events, student leaders have asked police officers to stop by to check on the crowd. Befriending police is useful because uniformed officers have a deterrent effect on radical activists. Potential disruptors think twice before committing a criminal act when the police are nearby, as long as they are not under any stand-down orders from elected officials.

Another potential danger is to have the platform taken over entirely. It is important to protect the microphone, especially during Q&A periods. In the past, I have witnessed several instances in which a dissenter hijacks the microphone and begins a monologue. Q&A periods are essential to the discussion, so I do not recommend cutting them, but one must take precautions to prevent someone from hijacking the event.

One solution is to have an usher control the microphone, without allowing an audience member to take it. This tactic can be awkward, but it is effective. If the attendee attempts to yank the microphone and keep it for themselves, the usher should be prepared to take it back. The second method is to screen questions beforehand using Twitter, Facebook, or email, and having a student read them to the speaker. This may not be the most desirable method, though, as it may give the appearance of a scripted event.

The most effective and natural way to handle a Q&A period is to have multiple microphones going around the room. This way, a sound technician can shut off the microphone if a disruptor hijacks the event. Ultimately, deplatforming can be beaten with enough early preparation.

Tearing Down Posters

Tearing down posters on college campuses is one of the Left's favorite tactics. When conservative clubs post flyers advertising meetings or events, leftist students routinely tear them down.

I have personally witnessed this at dozens of campuses. The first time was at UC Irvine. On this occasion, I was helping the Conservative Student Union host a speaker on Title IX. As the students were posting flyers, multiple people walked by and tore them down. I could not help but laugh at their audacity. To combat this, I have helped students set up sting operations. At Irvine, as the students were posting flyers, I sat nearby, observing the situation. Whenever someone would tear down a poster, I would jump up and film the incident. We attempted to hold them accountable by contacting administrators and the student life conduct council. However, we found that this took too long to be effective, especially when the administrators dragged their feet.

Since most of the time it is not possible to prevent leftist students from tearing down posters, it is better to set up a recruitment table and solicit members while advertising an event. Asking people for their contact information is much more efficient than posting or handing out flyers. It should be used regularly by any conservative activist who is committed to spreading their message.

Dealing with Hecklers

While tabling is more efficient than posting flyers, it also has its drawbacks. When tabling, a student or activist will be exposed to a variety of characters, many of whom will be indifferent to the conservative cause. But it also draws attention since many students are surprised that a conservative club openly tables. However, it sometimes leads to attempts by leftist students to instigate violence.

As mentioned earlier, it is important to befriend campus security and to call them if the need arises. However, it is not necessary to contact the authorities every time one decides to set up a recruitment table. Notifying the police beforehand should only be done if the tabling event touches on a controversial matter, or if the group routinely draws hecklers who turn violent. There will be times when leftist students become belligerent and flip the table, rip signs, or physically engage with the activists. One should always be ready to record an altercation. It is crucial to have a smartphone to record and upload a live video online.

This video can later be used to hold the protestors accountable and to garner media attention to combat the false notion that the Left is the victim. In many cases, the Left is the aggressor. Leftist students who have the gall to confront conservative students directly are more dangerous than those who tear down flyers. Holding these types of agitators accountable is far more worthwhile.

Unfortunately, there have been some incidents that get out of hand, such as one that occurred at Binghamton University in New York. There, the students found out just how fast a situation can deteriorate when the activist left is involved. On November 14, 2019, a Turning Point USA chapter was tabling to advertise one of their events. The situation quickly turned sour, and soon over two hundred people surrounded the students, demanding they take down their table and go home.[25] One young woman shouted in the face of a conservative activist. Another accused a student of being "white," and thus an oppressor. Antifa may pretend it is shutting down oppressive, racist speech, but the majority of left-wing activists I have encountered hold racist contempt for white people and minorities who are not reflexively liberal.

To make matters worse, the event the students were promoting was shut down within a minute of starting.[26] Two students were arrested in that incident. Yet the university's chapter of College Democrats released a statement condemning Turning Point and College Republicans for hosting the event.[27] Just as the guy who attacked me sat in handcuffs and whined to the police, leftist students who attack conservatives often pretend they are the victims.

This mob mentality scenario has played out time and time again. It happened to my friend Deepak Sahni in 2017. Deepak, like me, had been a conservative activist for several years, and started the California Freedom Project. He was helping some conservative students at Cal State Northridge while holding a sign that read, *Antifa is the new Fascism*. That was enough for over a hundred students to surround him and demand he leave campus.[28] Deepak told me the campus police had to escort him to his car because they feared for his safety.

At Sacramento State, a College Republicans club was tabling when the members found themselves surrounded by dozens of belligerent protesters.[29] At Ohio State, a right-wing commentator peacefully exercising her First Amendment rights was accosted by hundreds of leftist agitators who followed her around campus and demanded she leave.[30]

Throughout the country, events like these have occurred, while many others go unreported.

The best course of action in such a situation is to comply with the mob's demands. One's safety is more important than a tabling event. But one should also be sure to record the altercation if there is a safe means of doing so, because that footage can be used to expose the mob and hold individuals accountable. They may have won the battle, but they will not win against the universities' disciplinary boards. It is merely a matter of learning to pick one's fights.

Doxing

Doxing is the unlawful publication of identifying information about a person with the intent that the victim will be attacked, fired, ridiculed, or subjected to illegal behavior. In layman's terms, doxing is posting personal identifiable information in a public place so that those identified may be targets of crimes.

As alluded to earlier, these types of "speech" are not protected by the First Amendment. In *Brandenburg v. Ohio* (1969) the Supreme Court established a two-part test to allow the government to punish speech.[31] Under the test, speech may be banned only if it was intended to cause imminent lawless action and was likely to produce it. Doxing statutes meet the *Brandenburg* test because the doxing is intended to cause violence against the victim, which places the victim in imminent harm from those inspired by the threats. Additionally, doxing campaigns are likely to instigate violence against the peaceful victims. Doxing is thus unlawful speech.

Doxing is one of Antifa's favorite tactics. At neo-Nazi rallies, Antifa protesters take pictures of license plates to target the activists. However, this tactic is also used against innocent students, and has many times led to violence. For example, at Tulane University in Louisiana, several members of Young Americans for Liberty and Turning Point USA were doxed online, merely for having joined the right-wing groups. Not long afterwards, someone attempted to burn down their dorm room door.[32] At best, this act of attempted arson was a form of political intimidation. At worst, it reflected an intent to kill and a wanton disregard for human life.

Nevertheless, doxing is a recurring problem for conservative students. Take UT Austin, where an Antifa-affiliated group threatened to dox any incoming freshman who dared join a conservative club.[33] These were not mere threats, as they had doxed several conservative activists in the past, including student leaders. After pressure from the public, including myself, the university was prompted to act, and reached out to the state attorney general for legal options.[34] That said, as far as I can tell, no one has been held accountable. The public sometimes must demand justice to achieve it. It is up to people to demand that those in authority fulfill their duty to maintain civility in American society. Colleges have an obligation not to create a hostile environment that exposes their students to criminal threats.

Not only is doxing criminal behavior in many states, it may also be tortious under a theory of public disclosure of private facts. The tortious theory makes someone liable for publishing private information that is of no legitimate public concern. One's private residence and phone number, especially that of a private individual, may often be found to be of no public concern. Especially when the information is made public with the intent to cause harm to the victim. Thus, if one is doxed, a potential civil lawsuit may be brought against the perpetrator.

Doxing is hard to prepare against because it does not require direct confrontation. At the risk of being doxed myself, I do some of the following. First, I make sure to keep my address private. In many states, your residence can be easily accessed merely by requesting it from the secretary of state or voting registrar. Many states allow you to keep personal identifying information private, but regulations vary. It is best to contact the local voter registrar to inquire about potential options.

Second, I recommend maintaining different email accounts. I specifically sign up for various services using one address, but give out a different one to people who want to reach out to me. Having more than one email also prevents people from obtaining my log-in information. Services such as Google offer two-step verification protections that activate when someone attempts to hack into your account. To keep a phone number private, you can ask your phone provider not to be listed in directories. Also, Google offers a free phone number, which is easily accessible via the Google Voice app. Essentially, Google Voice allows you to have two different numbers on a single phone.

There are many ways to get around privacy walls on Facebook, Twitter, or Instagram. Thus, it is difficult to keep your social media accounts private. However, that does not mean you have to make it easy for a hacker. One way to hide personal information is to make your profile private. Some social media networks, by default, post your location with each post. It is essential to disable such a feature.

Receiving a random friend request also creates a risk. Far too many people add others without knowing them. Often, I think this practice is fine because social media can help people connect with others in the conservative movement. But just in case, I often send a message to a requesting person, asking why they want to connect.

If some of these actions seem paranoid, you are right. I learned to use these and other practices to maintain my privacy while I was an anarchist. They can be extreme at times. For example, I refused to post pictures of my face so Facebook did not have my image. However, if you really want to keep your information private, those are some starting points to consider.

Luckily, doxing is not a threat that most of us will face. Typically, those who are doxed are not regular conservative or libertarian people. The targets are generally government officials, college activists, and other conservative figures with a higher profile. People who attend only a few rallies to show support or volunteer in a campaign office face little threat of being doxed. It is the activists who routinely confront leftist radicals who must prepare against this threat.

Riots and Physical Confrontations

During the Occupy protests in the early 2010s, I remember reading an article on a radical website that was in favor of instigating riots. It recounted the story of an anarchist who supposedly began to break windows, when a peaceful protester confronted him and told him to stop. The article argued, "This peaceful protest is not our movement." Instead, the authors were in favor of direct action.

The truth is, there is little one can do to prepare for a riot. Often, riots are not started by large groups of people. Rather, they are sparked by a small number of individuals who are present during an otherwise peaceful protest, and try to move it toward mayhem and violence.

During the George Floyd protests, Americans saw this scenario play out in the early stages of the demonstrations. Multiple videos surfaced online and showed Antifa activists looting, breaking windows, starting fires, and attacking innocent bystanders while members of the local African American community decried the violence and begged for it to stop.[35] In more than one instance, peaceful African American activists even tried to protect the police from the Antifa rioters.[36] Unfortunately, their peaceful voices were drowned out by the violent riots started by Antifa.

The best thing you can do in case of a riot is to leave. It is better to avoid a situation that can lead to violence.

However, there have been times in which conservative activists find themselves in a precarious situation because they attended an event that at first appeared to be peaceful. It is crucial to rely on the police during a breach of peace, but it is also important to be careful not to rush a cop to ask to be protected. An officer may think you are one of the agitators and may push you back to maintain a scrimmage line. In any case, find people who are friendly and attempt to get away.

If one attends an event that could get out of hand, one should always have an exit plan. Something I used to do when I went to protests was to use Google Maps to know which houses I could jump into to evade detection if the need arose. At the very least, one needs to consider all the different exits in a building and arrive early to scope out the area. I have always been an athletic runner and practiced some parkour. Thus, at events, I tend to park off-site because I know how to get to my car safely. However, if this is not an option, find another one. The alternative scenario is being unable to get to your car, or worse, finding yourself driving a vehicle in the middle of a riot, as so many people found themselves doing amid the Floyd demonstrations.

In the case of physical confrontations not amounting to a riot, it is essential to read the room. The worst thing one can do is get into a fight. Remember, Antifa agitators are the ones starting the violence. If a conservative retaliates, the media will pretend it was an affray. The mainstream media wants to strip conservative victims of any legitimate sympathy. Sometimes self-defense is necessary. But use it only if the attacker does not cease. Even then, use force only to escape. Do not be drawn into a fight.

As discussed earlier, Hayden Williams was attacked without provocation at UC Berkeley. After he was punched in the face, he read the situation and realized Zach Greenberg was walking away, so he did not pursue a fight. This decision helped him because if he had been drawn into the battle that Zach wanted, the headlines would have read, *Political Brawl in Front of Sather Gate*, instead of, *Conservative Activist Attacked by Leftist Thug.*

Another thing Hayden did right was pull out his phone to record. And thankfully, others recorded a better angle. Without video documentation, the public would have never seen the attack, and Zachary would have gotten away with it. My recommendation is to download the Parachute app, or something similar. This app allows one to livestream with location, and the video is automatically saved online. The app can be incredibly useful because there may be situations in which leftists break or steal your phone.

Nathan Berning, a friend of mine and a former colleague at the Leadership Institute, can attest to the effectiveness of the Parachute app. His work as an activist took him to a protest that was being held on top of a roof. People started to notice he was not supportive, and began to accost him. Then someone noticed that he was filming, and said, "Let's film both of us at the same time." As Nathan agreed, someone snatched his phone and threw it over the ledge.[37]

Fortunately, his phone was running the Parachute app and recorded the entire interaction, including as it spiraled to the ground. Afterwards he was able to retrieve the phone, which was not completely broken. However, even had he not been able to find it, the video would have still been available online. In that event, Nathan used it to press charges against the student. A few months thereafter, thanks to the video evidence, the student was charged and convicted of criminal misconduct and ordered to pay restitution.

The most important thing to do in a riot or physical altercation is to keep safe. Do not give up your life or compromise your safety for the movement. It is OK to lose the battle in order to fight again and win the culture war.

Blocking Traffic

Antifa and other radical groups like to block traffic because it creates a lot of attention. However, it is one of their most unpopular tactics. Ultimately, Antifa needs to maintain the sympathy of regular people. When Antifa picks a target, it is typically one that most people can rally against. In this case, the blocking adversely affects the general public. It is, thus, a loser tactic. Nevertheless, it is worth understanding it in case you ever find yourself trapped in your car during a street-blocking action.

This tactic requires a lot of people, and it is abnormally dangerous. I never did this, but I have seen videos and met people who have performed the blockade. Typically, demonstrators link arms to create a human chain and intercept cars driving down the street. Most drivers, being decent people, naturally stop to avoid hitting the demonstrators. Unfortunately, there have been some accidents as a result.

I cannot stress how foolish this tactic is for everyone concerned. It creates an unreasonable risk of harm for both protesters and drivers. Still, the best way to respond is to hunker down inside one's car. It may be annoying, but the protesters have the drivers in a vulnerable position. It is better to lose an hour of one's time than to injure someone and possibly serve time in jail for vehicular manslaughter. This is especially the case since the tactic will ultimately backfire.

A perfect example of this tactic gone wrong occurred in 2019 when the leftist UK group Extinction Rebellion blocked London's public transport network during rush hour.[38] Extinction Rebellion is a left-wing environmental group that uses nonviolent tactics to get their political message across. But by annoying the heck out of normal Londoners trying to get to work, their message was overshadowed by images of commuters pulling the activists down from atop train cars so normal life could resume. Later on, Extinction Rebellion was forced to apologize. Similarly, the tactic of blocking streets and highways in America will eventually backfire for Black Lives Matter—as long as most people stay in their cars and avoid escalation.

The dynamic changes when it is no longer about blocking traffic, but about surrounding a specific vehicle. In Austin, Texas, a predictable tragedy occurred when a driver was surrounded by BLM demonstrators. Among them was Garrett Foster, a libertarian activist who was supportive of Black Lives Matter.[39] Within seconds, multiple shots were fired from more than one weapon, killing Foster on the spot. In a video of this episode, people are seen running, and a woman is heard sobbing. Putting aside whether the driver acted reasonably under the circumstances, Garrett's death was caused by this reckless tactic of blocking off the highway, which is a trademark of Antifa and Black Lives Matter.

I am not an attorney and am in no position to give legal advice on the matter. However, *The Blaze* published an article a few years ago that offers some possible scenarios in which a driver may be legally justified in using his car in self-defense.[40] There are a few points that deserve to be highlighted:

- A car is widely considered to be a deadly weapon when used to touch another person intentionally. The driver must therefore have perceived a reasonable and imminent threat to life or serious bodily harm.

- Even if justified in driving past protestors, one must exercise due care, meaning one should not speed through recklessly, but slowly push people aside to get free.

- Even if one successfully defends oneself in criminal court, a protester who is injured may still sue civilly for any damages incurred.

- Statutes vary from state to state. Thus, one should consult with an attorney.

The best nonlegal personal advice I can give involves a topic I discussed in an earlier section of the book—choosing where to park. I tend to park off-site, which prevents me from being surrounded by Antifa or other radical protesters. If possible, arrive at an event early, park a few streets away, and make an evacuation plan in case things turn sour.

In general, when dealing with Antifa, there is one crucial point that everyone needs to consider. Antifa wants confrontation.

Whenever possible, it is best to avoid them. The only predictable result of physically engaging Antifa is that more members will join its cause. If you find yourself in a situation in which you are threatened with bodily harm, use whatever reasonable means necessary to escape and find safety. But never escalate the situation.

Antifa thrives on violence and scrimmages. What Antifa activists fear most is failing in their mission but being punished anyway.

Hold them accountable by surveilling them and giving the information to the police or other authorities. If they attempt to run you off campus, record the incident and set the record straight, because the mainstream media rarely reports the truth that conservatives are under attack. If they want to go low, we will go high.

In a battle of ideas, violence will not win.

CHAPTER 5

ANTIFA'S FUEL

I am from Southern California, one of the most liberal parts of the country. By the time I was ready to graduate from college, I believed I had seen the worst of liberal bias in the classroom. But I was yet to see the full severity of the partisanship that plagues countless institutions of higher learning. I would soon find out that what happened to me was not unique to Southern California. Professors across the country teach their students to hate conservatives for mere political disagreements. What's worse, college administrators are often complicit in creating an intolerant environment that is openly hostile to ideological diversity. In effect, institutions of higher education brainwash students by creating an echo chamber of self-righteous ideologies. The either-or mentality that these administrations promote has created a culture in which Antifa and its violent mentality now thrive.

While I was once a leftist, I was still new to the leftist bias that is harbored by so many colleges and universities.

During the summer of 2015, I accepted an invitation to attend the Leadership Institute's field representative training. I had been involved with the Leadership Institute for two years by then, as they helped me with my political activism. While my friend Adam was no longer the regional field coordinator, I trusted the Institute to help me define my next step. The job of Leadership Institute field representatives is to travel outside their home states to fight against liberal bias and defend conservative students so they do not go through what I experienced at Citrus College. First, though, it's necessary to complete an intensive two-week training course in Arlington, Virginia. As soon as I received the invitation, I handed in my two weeks' notice.

Over fifty candidates had been invited from around the country, and in talking to them, I was surprised to hear stories acutely similar to mine. Some candidates told me they had been kicked off campus, their events had been shut down, or that they had a tough time getting recognized by the school. In a few situations, leftist students and professors had stolen or destroyed their property. At the time, such incidents were rarer than they are now, but they sometimes did occur. I was not entirely sure what I was getting myself into, but I knew I wanted to help students start a conversation, just like Adam once helped me.

While I had experienced liberal bias on my own campus, some of the training seemed far-fetched. I did not think I would get kicked off campus for merely setting up a table. And if it did happen, I thought it was only a few schools. At that time, I thought leftist administrators mobilized against conservative activists only if they were doing something controversial. As I would soon learn, the Left thinks everything conservatives do is controversial.

The training consisted of both lecture and field exercises in which regional field coordinators could monitor us to be sure we were competent to stand up to the Left on campus. After a week and a half, thirty candidates were selected and assigned to different states. I was assigned to Colorado, which was coveted by several candidates. Since the state is in the middle of the country, I expected the political environment to be more tolerant toward conservatives and libertarians. I was right, in part. People in Colorado are much nicer and less standoffish than the Southern Californians I was used to. However, the job of field representative showed me that colleges in Colorado were a different story.

The day I began my work as a field representative, I was kicked off a community college campus in Northern Colorado. Then the same happened in Boulder the next day. By the end of the semester, I had been kicked out of a dozen schools simply for trying to talk to students in a public place. Far too many colleges and universities violate the First Amendment protections of students who are merely attempting to engage peacefully in civil discussion. It was these same kinds of free speech violations that prompted me and Vinny to sue Citrus College in 2014. Yet they are occurring at countless schools around the country. The more I worked with conservative students, the more egregious examples I found.

Once, I helped a conservative student start a club that he decided to name the America Club. The kid was generally conservative, but not all that political, nor were his views controversial. I think the reason he decided to start the club was just so he could meet more like-minded people. However, during a meeting with a college administrator, the campus bureaucrat began to question the name and intentions of the club. He claimed the name was not inclusive of all students and might make people feel unsafe, especially those—like me—who came from Latin America.

At first, I was taken aback. As a trained activist, I began to record the conversation. We explained that the club was meant to celebrate American heritage and the Constitution, but he did not seem convinced. When he began speaking, I realized he was attempting to dissuade the student from starting the club. He made excuses for not approving the club immediately, like he typically did for most clubs. Unfortunately, before I was able to upload the video online, my phone got wet, so I lost all my data. Had I used the Parachute app, I would have been able to expose his leftist bias.

Fortunately, the club was approved a few days later. But it should have gotten the stamp of approval on the spot. That kind of delay is enough to have a chilling effect on the free speech and assembly rights of conservative students. Often, campus administrators use their power to stall and block conservative student initiatives. In this instance, the infraction may have been minor, but sometimes it takes litigation to force schools to respect the rights of all their students.

The Supreme Court in *Grayned v. City of Rockford* (1972) did give government agencies, including colleges, some leeway to restrict speech. These are called the time, place, and manner restrictions, and they are constitutionally permissible as long as the rules are applied neutrally and serve an agency's interest—in this case, if the speech unreasonably disturbs the school's educational process. For example, a professor is constitutionally protected in denying a student's right to free speech if the student intends to stand in front of the class and protest, because that would disrupt the professor's lecture. However, it would be unconstitutional if professors allowed liberal students to protest in that manner, but then punished conservatives for doing the same.

In my experience, I have found that "neutral" policies are not enforced with a blind eye. These restrictive rules are often weaponized to silence conservative thought.

Take the Young Americans for Liberty chapter I helped at UC Berkeley. For a free speech ball event, the libertarian students were using an electrical outlet on the side of the building to inflate their giant beach ball. This outlet was routinely used by other students without any problem. However, as soon as administrators saw the libertarian students were using it to perform a liberty-minded activism project, they were told to stop, or campus security would be called. Administrators have every right to prevent students from using that outlet. The problem arises when they give liberal students special treatment and threaten conservative students with expulsion and sanctions.

For this student group, liberal bias was also institutionalized. Not long after this incident, another field rep and I helped them sue the university for being denied official recognition.[1] The administrative board reasoned that the club was too "similar" to other existing conservative and libertarian clubs. Of course, the school does not use that reasoning to deny liberal organizations. After this clear violation, the school was forced to settle.

This scenario plays itself out time and time again throughout the country. At Worchester State in Massachusetts, a Turning Point USA chapter was denied chartering because it was a conservative club.[2] And when I was at Citrus College, the student government unsuccessfully tried to block a right-wing club from chartering. Since I was a student government officer, I had a vote in that controversy. Numerous leftist students publicly tried to force me to abstain because I was friends with the student who started the club. I have witnessed countless universities using their so-called content-neutral policies to shut down conservative speech while affording left-leaning student organizations a myriad of resources.

When conservatives attempt to exercise the same rights, they are threatened with legal and procedural sanctions.

A more blatant example comes from UC San Marcos, where a regional field coordinator named Nathan Fatal was helping a Students for Life chapter.[3] The group applied for $500 in school funding for an event that was denied. Nathan thought it sounded fishy, so he helped the student to investigate. They soon found that a feminist and LGBTQ organization had received almost $300,000 in student fees. In addition, the entire funding process was conducted in closed-door meetings, which made it difficult for conservative students to appeal the decisions. Fortunately, thanks to Nathan's help, the students were connected with the Alliance Defending Freedom, a pro bono law firm that filed and won a lawsuit against the school. Throughout my time with the Leadership Institute, I have connected dozens of students with pro bono legal assistance.

One of the most prominent cases I was involved in was at Los Angeles Pierce College in Southern California. In this instance, activist Andrew Di Giovanna and I helped student Kevin Shaw pass out pocket U.S. Constitutions when administrators attempted to do what so many others have done, confining us to a small "free speech" area on campus in violation of our constitutional rights. Andrew and I connected the student with the Foundation for Individual Rights in Education (FIRE), another pro bono legal group, which led to yet another lawsuit and eventually drew the attention of the Department of Justice.[4] Luckily, the case led to a favorable settlement. However, conservatives and libertarians should not have to sue to assert their basic rights.

The systematic bias against conservative and libertarian students likely stems from the ideological makeup of university faculty, who openly promote an us-versus-them mentality. A study in 2016, found that liberal professors outnumber conservative professors twelve to one.[5] This uneven ideological makeup has led higher education to become an echo chamber in which conservative voices are silenced or forced out. But this bias does not stop with academics; it also gives rise to more antisocial behavior. There have been many instances of professors becoming so comfortable in their positions that they start showing their true colors.

In 2018, a professor at Georgetown University tweeted that conservatives "deserve miserable deaths."[6] The director of Northeastern University's Women's, Gender, and Sexuality Studies Program claimed women have every right to hate men.[7] At UT Austin, a professor claimed that Trump and all his supporters were Nazis.[8] A UC Berkeley instructor claimed that rural Americans are "bad people" who "deserve to live uncomfortable lives."[9]

This type of language is not productive. It serves only to divide and intimidate. Author Mark Bray has argued that Antifa ought to fight against oppressive language, but he would likely refuse to condemn sexist and classist rhetoric promulgated by left-wing faculty when they target conservatives.

This hatred of conservatives is not confined to the professors' personal lives. Liberal bias often appears in the classroom. At Brookdale Community College, a sociology professor screamed, "Fuck your life," at a conservative student.[10] In California, an Orange Coast College professor claimed Trump's election was an "act of terrorism."[11] And when the COVID-19 pandemic forced schools to move online, leftist professors across the nation worried that their controversial lectures would be recorded.[12] Their concerns were well-founded. During one online lecture, a professor from East Carolina University was caught calling Fox News "anti-immigrant," and suggested that the founder of its parent company was racist.[13]

I have been in classes where professors rail against conservatives and right-wing commentators, which makes conservative students afraid to speak out. There are examples of this behavior in every state, and the list seems to grow with each semester.

A university has a vested interest in promoting ideological diversity. Such systematic bias hinders learning for both conservative and liberal students. Conservative students are subjected to ideological bullying simply for not believing the same platitudes that liberals espouse. Liberal bias also does a disservice to liberal students because they are ill-prepared to defend their beliefs when they go out into the real world. In short, colleges and universities today teach students what to think, not how to think.

Professors have every right to hold personal opinions about politics. When they teach courses that involve political issues, I think it is fair for them to express their views. However, this is not the same as being biased. Bias in the classroom means presenting one's opinions as infallible while belittling opposing views. Professors have an ethical and indeed contractual responsibility to treat their students fairly. But more than that, they have a duty not to create a hostile learning environment. Leftist professors frequently breach this duty when they intimidate conservative students merely for having different opinions. When professors teach from personal bias, it creates an environment which helps to nurture the Antifa tactics and ideology.

Over the past several decades, more and more professors have taught from a position of bias. The consequence has been to escalate from contentious debates to physical confrontations between professors and students. At Cal State Fullerton, a professor punched a conservative student during a pro-Trump event.[14] During protests at the University of Missouri, Professor Melissa Click was charged with assault after calling for "muscle" to remove student journalists from the rally.[15] If the system does not work for the Left, they are willing to use force to bend and break it.

If professors and administrators do not succeed in silencing conservative thought through the system of indoctrination and enforcement they have created on many campuses, some will take it upon themselves to escalate situations. This type of escalation teaches students that hurting others for a political cause is not only permissible, it is necessary. Indeed, some professors proclaim that Antifa is a form of self-defense.[16] This explains why many of the people I met in Antifa were college students. For better or worse, American colleges and universities serve as laboratories for radical thought and action. For decades, leftist professors have promoted bias against conservatives in the classroom. Their bias planted seeds in the minds of thousands of young college students, and now many believe political violence is justifiable. After decades of leftist indoctrination, Antifa's philosophy is no longer a fringe ideology, but a mainstream danger in American politics. The results are clear to see in the recent BLM protests in many American cities.

Although colleges and universities are the primary sources for breeding this intolerant view of the world, they are not alone. The liberal media and several prominent activists also push this violent mentality. In August 2019, protestors gathered around Kentucky Senator Mitch McConnell's home and shouted death threats. Very few networks covered the protests outside his home, and the media downplayed the nastiness of the liberal protestors. Thus, MSNBC's Chris Hayes characterized the protests as peaceful. Meanwhile, his guest, attorney Elie Mystal, called for people to march to the homes of Trump donors with "pitchforks and torches."[17]

The mainstream media routinely ignores violence against conservatives, while often promoting unlawful behavior. During the BLM riots, the mainstream media held to the line that the demonstrations were "mostly peaceful," ignoring or refusing to report on the out-of-control violence that erupted in many American cities, under guise of legitimate protests. This refusal provided cover for violent agitators and plainly encouraged them.

In some cases, the liberal mainstream actively promotes Antifa agitators and groups. CNN contributor Kamau Bell conducted an insider interview with a current member of Antifa in his documentary series, *The United States of Shades.*[18] During the interview, the activist proudly recounted pounding another person at a protest. She also pulled out her multiple brass knuckles and knives, which prompted Bell to laugh as if political violence was all a big joke. She also had a handful of flyers that contained the personal information of an ICE agent, which she used to dox him by holding them up for the camera. An attorney at CNN likely saw what Bell had done and told the producers to blur the image, as it would have been a crime to dox an ICE officer on national television. That interview was nothing but a puff piece for Antifa, which obviously served to encourage the growth of the movement.

Bell also highlighted the Redneck Revolt, which, as I mentioned earlier, is a self-identified Antifa organization. At first, he expressed confusion and asked why left-wing agitators would support the Second Amendment, which is considered a right-wing issue. That confusion ended when he began to see them as allies and went on to call them the "good guys."[19] Among the Redneck Revolt members he interviewed was Willem van Spronsen, the self-identified Antifa member who attacked ICE agents in Washington State, with a rifle and incendiary devices.[20] Bell may pretend to be a reputable reporter, but his documentary series was an irresponsible act of partisan journalism.

One can always count on the mainstream media to act as a professional PR team to justify Antifa violence.

Colleges and the mainstream media are not the only ones responsible for promoting Antifa's mentality and methods. There are some personalities who, while not directly promoting Antifa's violence, help create the culture in which Antifa thrives. Environmental activist Greta Thunberg is a prime example.

Thunberg is the Left's darling when it comes to environmental issues. In a passionate speech at the U.N., she yelled, "How dare you!" at the older generation, shaming those who would not support her legislative agenda.[21] At the ripe age of sixteen, she was also named *Time Magazine*'s Person of the Year.[22] While some find her vigor inspiring, I see through her hateful ideology. When I was Greta's age, I started my political journey when I refused to stand for the pledge of allegiance. Although I mostly found support from fellow students, whenever someone criticized me, I would use Greta's line, "How dare you," while I lectured them about supporting "American propaganda." I believed as Greta does that if you are not with me, you are the enemy.

This either-or mentality blinded me, and it is, in part, why I eventually joined the antifascist movement. The first step to radicalization is to dehumanize a political opponent. One can then paint them as evil incarnate. Once an opponent is no longer viewed as human, he becomes an easier target for intimidation and violence.

I was fortunate enough to grow out of this false oppositional mentality. Unfortunately, many people carry it with them beyond their teens. For example, in 2019, a college student disrupted an event by the Georgetown University College Republicans that sought to bring a different perspective to the climate change debate.[23] The student entered the room and used a bullhorn to disrupt a peaceful program, which prompted the police to come and stop him. At first glance, this may seem like the act of an immature child. But it goes to a deeper problem in America. I do not think that Greta Thunberg intends to radicalize people. Unfortunately, her apocalyptic mindset gives left-wing liberals an excuse to lock themselves in an echo chamber and lash out at anyone who has a different point of view.

What makes it all worse is that so many elected officials promote Antifa. Former Minnesota Democratic representative Keith Ellison tweeted a selfie with Mark Bray's violent manifesto, stating he had "just found the book that strike[s] fear in the heart of @realDonaldTrump."[24] Ellison was also the Democratic National Committee deputy chairman, and in 2019, left his position in Congress to serve as Minnesota's attorney general.

Minnesota seems to have a problem with extremist politicians who support Antifa—like Democratic State Representative Aisha Gomez. In October 2019, Gomez was seen in all-black clothing among Antifa protesters outside a Donald Trump rally. Amid the George Floyd riots, Minneapolis City Councilmember Jeremiah Ellison, who happens to be Minnesota Attorney General Keith Ellison's son, openly declared his support for Antifa on Twitter.[25] Surprisingly, Far-Left Democratic Congresswoman Ilhan Omar declared, that while the protests were valid, the destruction of property was not.[26]

Yet another example of elected officials defending Antifa comes from Boston. In late 2019, Boston Police rightfully arrested several Antifa activists for beating up some rallygoers. As they were facing charges, Representatives Alexandria Ocasio-Cortez and Ayanna Pressley began a campaign to fundraise and bail them out of jail. These people are elected officials who are supposed to represent their constituents. However, they seem to have more loyalty to a failed extremist ideology than to the American people.

Then there are politicians who refuse to hold criminal activists responsible for their actions. First in line is Portland Mayor Ted Wheeler, who has failed to police Rose City Antifa. The lack of leadership Wheeler has displayed is why Antifa routinely shows up in this city to cause destruction and chaos. In 2018, for example, Wheeler refused to arrest Antifa agitators who were blocking and directing traffic.[27] Antifa appeared to have more authority than the police in this scenario. Then in 2019, ahead of a Proud Boys rally, a Ted Wheeler event hosted a speaker who supported Antifa's tactics and claimed Antifa was merely defending the city against white supremacists.[28] It's no surprise that Texas Senator Ted Cruz called for a federal investigation into Mayor Wheeler's failure to keep the peace for political reasons.[29]

No one should be surprised that some of the worst violence in the country after George Floyd's death occurred in Portland, Oregon. It was due to Mayor Wheeler's complete lack of leadership and backbone that his city was under siege by Antifa for over two months. Almost every night, Antifa terrorists destroyed property and intimidated local residents. The PNW Youth Liberation Front, an antifascist network in Portland, also tried to set up its own autonomous zone like Seattle's CHAZ.[30] Fortunately, the local police were able to prevent the occupation.

In the end, Mayor Wheeler did not want to take any responsibility for the violence. Instead, he blamed President Trump and his decision to send federal agents to protect federal buildings.[31] As Wheeler said, "The best thing they can do is stay inside their building, or leave Portland altogether."[32] While Wheeler may wish to pretend that Antifa organizers were victims of police brutality, videos clearly show that Antifa was instigating altercations with federal police. One video shows two Antifa activists attempting to imprison U.S. marshals inside a building by blocking the only exit while trying to set fire to the building.[33] When one of the officers broke free, one of the agitators began swinging a hammer, and hit him repeatedly. About ten other officers then rush out of the building to help him, while the second agitator abandons his accomplice. Had Mayor Wheeler held Rose City Antifa accountable for its crimes when he had the chance, there would have been no need for federal intervention.

Fortunately, the months of nightly violence in Portland have exposed Antifa's true intentions. On August 1st, while some Antifa agitators were ripping protective boarding off of buildings, others were setting a pile of Bibles ablaze.[34] This is a strange way to honor George Floyd, a Christian man who, after several run-ins with the law, turned to Christ in 2013.[35] But Antifa does not care about his Christian values. Instead, Antifa wants to destroy everything that America stands for, including Christianity.

It all goes back to college campuses. In 2017, Young Americans for Freedom at California State University, Los Angeles (CSULA), planned to host Ben Shapiro. Before the event, a professor physically threatened the student organizers, and ultimately the school defended the professor's conduct.[36] But what is worse is that on the day of the event, the school's police received a stand-down order that prevented them from stopping the altercations that later ensued.[37]

Ben and the students wanted the event to continue so as not to let free speech die that day. So as fights broke out, some people were smuggled inside the auditorium through the back. Unfortunately, the plan did not last long, as the agitators realized what was happening and blocked the doors with their bodies. These radical students imprisoned everyone inside, including myself. Then a few minutes into Ben's speech, someone pulled the fire alarm to create panic among those inside. Fortunately, everyone remained calm.

After the event, Ben wanted to go out and speak to the crowd, but the police urged him not to, as that could start a riot. Fortunately, I made it out without being noticed by the leftist mob. The first thing I did was walk toward the front doors, where I saw about twenty-five students pressing their bodies against the entrance. I asked a student nearby what was going on. She told me the students were protesting the person inside the auditorium because he hated Jews. For those who may not understand the irony—Ben Shapiro is Jewish. I am certain she did not even know Ben's name. All this happened because the people in authority refused to enforce laws on the books that would have prevented the chaos.

An even more egregious example of a stand-down order comes from Evergreen College in Olympia, Washington. In this instance, the Far-Right fascist was actually the school's progressive biology professor, Bret Weinstein. It all began in 2016, when Professor Weinstein expressed his dissent on a resolution that encouraged dialogue on race and equality.[38] Reportedly, Weinstein's reason for dissenting was the lack of discussion during the drafting and adoption of the resolution. Asking questions and seeking a peaceful discussion is enough for the Left to brand you a fascist. The professor began receiving hatred from leftist students, as if he was the scum of the earth, and according to Weinstein, the school's president was on the mob's side.[39] One day, the police called and informed him that a mob of fifty students was stopping cars and searching for him. Unfortunately, the police could not protect him, as the college president had issued a stand-down order.[40]

Stand-down orders issued by college presidents to campus police have become all too common. But they are a sign that Antifa and its leftist mentality is no longer a fringe ideology; it is mainstream, and it exists at all levels of government.

As we have said, Antifa is not an organization, it is a reactionary movement that serves as an umbrella for left-wing radical groups and activists. Its violent ideology is fueled by colleges and universities that promote an us-versus-them mentality in the classroom. Antifa's rage is then sparked by the mainstream media's false sense of outrage. And while politicians have the power to extinguish the flames, they often refuse to act because they falsely believe Antifa serves their political agenda.

Antifa existed before our highly partisan culture. However, it is a combination of these groups that have launched it seemingly overnight, from obscurity to mainstream prominence.

CHAPTER 6

IS ANTIFA A DOMESTIC TERRORIST GROUP?

I am routinely asked whether Antifa should be declared a domestic terrorist organization. At first, I refused to do so and would bluntly say that I did not think it warranted such a designation. I mainly took this stance because I knew that kids under eighteen are often involved in the movement. At seventeen, I was the youngest of my group. But by the time I left, there were other kids younger than me. Eventually, I abandoned this reasoning because I realized ISIS also uses child soldiers.

Notwithstanding, I still resisted the classification because when I think of terrorism, I think of ISIS, Al-Qaeda, bombings, beheadings, armed conflict, or planned intimidation on a large scale. Whereas, with Antifa I think of punches, burning trash cans, and destruction of property. Thus, it appears there is a clear distinction between the two groups. However, I eventually concluded that ISIS and Antifa merely represent two forms of terrorism. The lethality of each group is not important to the underlying aim—namely, the use of violence for a political purpose.

I also resisted the Antifa classifications because ISIS and Al-Qaeda are organizations with formal leadership, ranks, and a stated mission. Antifa consists of loosely connected groups with no official leadership and a vague mission to fight "fascists." However, a description of the modern jihad can help demonstrate how Al-Qaeda and ISIS do share a commonality with Antifa.

For the last several decades, there has been a debate as to the definition of jihad. Some people believe it to have military connotations, while others believe it to be in the nature of a personal struggle to become closer to Allah.[1] That debate, and the true meaning of jihad, are not important for this analogy. What is important is that some extremist groups subjectively believe jihad to mean fighting against nonbelievers.

Antifa works in a similar fashion. Anyone who subjectively believes in the military definition of jihad can create an independent cell to terrorize those they proclaim to be nonbelievers. Similarly, anyone who believes in the Antifa ethos can create an independent cell to terrorize those they proclaim to be fascists. While their degree of violence may differ, they work through similarly structured cells in order to terrorize innocent people.

It should go without saying that not all Muslims believe in the minority view of the military-esque jihad. Similarly, not all who are antifascist believe in using military-style tactics. Kind of like me. I am still an antifascist; I am just not part of Antifa.

Whether Antifa should be declared a terrorist organization was answered by President Trump after Antifa orchestrated riots across the country in the wake of George Floyd's death.[2] Additionally, Attorney General William P. Barr stated, "The violence instigated and carried out by Antifa and other similar groups in connection with the rioting is domestic terrorism and will be treated accordingly."[3] Many Americans rejoiced and now believe that Antifa will be dealt with accordingly.

Unfortunately, the United States still has no process, statutes, or guidelines to designate domestic groups as terrorist organizations. Thus, while every sensible American may rightfully call Antifa a domestic terrorist organization, that has no real meaning in law because the category does not legally exist.

However, the United States does have a way to classify domestic terrorist acts. In the United States, terrorist acts are defined in Title 22, Chapter 38 of the United States Code, as "premeditated, politically motivated violence perpetrated against noncombatant targets by subnational groups or clandestine agents."[4] The department of justice has used similar domestic statutes to crack down on ecoterrorists in the 1990s, and Antifa will likely be treated similarly. Attorney General Barr will likely tackle the Antifa threat like the ecoterrorists of the 1990s because it should come as no surprise to anyone that Antifa meets each element of that law.

The first legal challenge to meet is the element of premeditation. A terrorist act cannot be a spontaneous or sporadic criminal act; it must be carefully planned or thought out beforehand.

Antifa plots are often carefully planned out well in advance. One of the clearest examples comes from the Antifascist Coalition in D.C., and its attempts to shut down President Trump's inauguration on January 20, 2017. This coalition included groups like the International Socialists of the World (IWW), Refuse Fascism, and the Metropolitan Anarchist Coordinating Council. Several days before the inauguration, these Antifa agitators met in secret to plan their strategy. However, among them was a Project Veritas undercover journalist who captured their plan to shut down D.C.

traffic, including the D.C. Metro.[5] In these meetings, Antifa agitators specifically conspired to violate 18 U.S.C. 1992 statute, which makes it a criminal terrorist act to perpetrate attacks against mass transportation systems.

Another statutory element is motive: the attacks must be politically motivated. There is no doubt that Antifa attacks meet this standard. The Antifa members in D.C. were specifically motivated against President-Elect Donald Trump. But there is also the time several Antifa agitators attacked journalist Andy Ngo.[6] Andy Ngo is an independent journalist in Portland, who has devoted himself to exposing Antifa attacks around the country. In one protest, he was merely among a crowd, recording the criminal acts of Rose City Antifa, when he was attacked and beaten by Antifa agitators. The black bloc surrounded him, kicked him, threw milkshakes at him, and stole his video equipment, causing him serious injury. In an op-ed, Professor Stanislav Vysotsky from the University of Wisconsin–Whitewater, claimed Antifa attacked Andy Ngo because he was a conservative journalist who posed a threat to minority communities.[7] He thus attempted to justify the attacks by claiming they were in self-defense. While he misunderstands or distorts what constitutes an act of self-defense, at least he concedes that Antifa's attacks are politically motivated. Thus, the element of motive can be easily established.

The third element requires that the victim be a noncombatant. While Antifa has been known to attack government forces, such attacks are not technically terrorist acts under the statute, mainly because police officers are not considered *noncombatants*. Thus, Antifa must attack civilians to meet the statute's definition. Antifa routinely attacks civilians, including Andy Ngo, thus satisfying the third element.

Lastly, the statute requires the perpetrator be a "subnational group or clandestine agent." An organized national group does not sponsor Antifa, but if one did, such attacks would more aptly be classified as acts of war. Antifa's subnational status helps establish the last element of the statute. Further, Antifa activists conceal their identities to evade capture by police. In the case of Andy Ngo, the attackers concealed their identities. This would fit the definition of clandestine agents, which would be another way of establishing the last element in the terrorism statute.

Even as Antifa activists are prosecuted with domestic terrorist statutes, Antifa itself is still not an officially designated terrorist organization because the label does not exist. Thus, until the United States establishes a model for labeling domestic terrorist groups, the correct statement is that Antifa is a movement that engages in terrorist acts. Once a procedure to classify domestic terrorist groups is established, Antifa groups will most likely fit the bill. However, this raises the question as to whether Antifa itself can be declared a domestic terror group.

When President Trump and Attorney General Barr declared their intention to classify Antifa demonstrators as domestic terrorists, pundits were quick to point out the unprecedented nature of the measure. Many argued that domestic terror designations are inconsistent with the First Amendment because classifying domestic groups as terrorists would criminalize their freedom of association. As Arizona State University Professor Peter Bergen wrote, "Of course, should an American citizen commit a crime in service of her extremist beliefs, she can be prosecuted for that crime, but she can't be prosecuted for merely belonging to the group, no matter how objectionable its views might be."[8]

To his credit, Professor Bergen highlights an essential point. If Antifa is declared a domestic terror group, its activists cannot be arrested immediately, because criminal law requires a person to commit a volitional act. Merely harboring improper thoughts, ill will, or ill-intent does not, and should never, warrant the force of the United States Government. The United States Constitution and common law rightfully prevent the police from arresting Antifa activists, even if they show up in black bloc, as long as they do not engage in violence.

Also, since Antifa members are presumably American citizens, they should be afforded due process, which means finding probable cause, charging the suspect with a crime, and then having a jury of their peers judge them. This process is already how local governments deal with the Antifa threat. For example, during Donald Trump's presidential inauguration, over two hundred protestors were arrested and charged with rioting.[9] Every Antifa activist was rightly afforded due process and was considered innocent until proven guilty.

However, if Antifa is slapped with a domestic terrorist label, once a member is convicted, it would allow the government to take the fight directly to Antifa and its network. In such a case, the terrorist classification would allow the prosecution to seek further penalties after a conviction. Convicting an Antifa terrorist would then allow the government to investigate his connections and affiliates. This label would expose the Antifa network to law enforcement.

The result would be similar to using the Racketeer Influenced and Corrupt Organizations Act (RICO) against Antifa. RICO was passed in the 1970 to take down the Mafia, and "makes it illegal for a person to participate in the affairs of an enterprise that engages in 'racketeering activities'...which include 'crimes like arson, robbery, fraud, and money laundering.'"[10]

In effect, it would become illegal to be a member of Antifa, not due to punishing the ideology of the movement, but because Antifa participates in racketeering activities. Classifying Antifa as a domestic terrorist group would be inconsistent with the First Amendment only if it were used as a club to punish mere membership. Instead, the terrorist label is a tool to connect the dots in the Antifa conspiracy, which would be constitutionally permissible.

Some critics have told me that the real domestic terrorists are white supremacists, the KKK, the NSM, or other hate groups. My response is, "Them, too."

There are far too many groups that terrorize communities. Some are worse than others. Nevertheless, each of them is an evil expression of hate. Americans should never tolerate a hateful group that senselessly attacks Muslims, Jewish people, Christians, conservatives, or liberals. Members of Antifa believe themselves to be the defenders of freedom, but that is not true. Antifa is simply another hate group that throws temper tantrums to weed out ideological opponents and defectors. A domestic terrorist classification would not be a tool merely to fight Antifa, but to challenge all groups that terrorize people for a political purpose. A domestic terrorist label would help protect the rights afforded to all Americans.

Another objection I often hear is that not everyone in Antifa has engaged in political violence, so a domestic terrorist label would be unwarranted. I sympathize with this claim. In fact, I never engaged in any physical altercations while in Antifa. Yet this is not the only defining characteristic of Antifa.

In February 2020, conservative students at the University of Massachusetts–Amherst invited me to their campus to participate in a Change My Mind event made popular by conservative commentator Steven Crowder. This event consists of one person sitting behind a table with a controversial statement on a placard, and inviting others to change his or her mind. Some of the provocative statements that Crowder has stood behind include, "Affirmative Action is Racist," or "Hate Speech Isn't Real." These events are effective for Crowder, who has debated a multitude of people over the past several years. At my event, I sat behind a sign that read, "Antifa is Terrorism."

We could have not picked a worse day to do the event since it was February in Massachusetts, and the temperature was below freezing. The cold got to me quickly, and we were out for only an hour. Yet even though we were on campus only for a short time, we received a lot of interest. Some conversations were constructive; others were not productive at all. The first interaction we had was within five minutes of setting up, as a girl passed by the sign and took a picture of us. One of the students invited her to come and talk to us. Her reply was to say, "You're fucking wrong!" and stormed away.

The first person who approached the table was neither conservative nor liberal. He was simply curious about who we were and what Antifa was. I started giving him a brief history of Antifa, when two people approached and stood near him. One was a liberal student, but the second, as I soon found out, was a self-proclaimed Antifa activist. Both were respectful throughout the conversation, and neither of them objected to the brief history I recounted. For the next twenty minutes, the nonpolitical student heard me debate the two left-wing students. Fortunately, he decided that he agreed with me.

The self-proclaimed Antifa activist (let's call him Dave) did make some points worth considering. His first objection was that Antifa has never killed anyone, which I dismissed, giving example after example of Antifa killings, including the Italian Red Brigade and the Mexican anarchist group that murdered a scientist in 2011. He then began to argue the number of killings committed by those Antifa is fighting, but it was clear he had lost the point and was forced to change the subject.

Dave's second objection was that the United States government should be considered a terrorist organization since it has killed innocent people during war. My basic argument was that there is a difference between Antifa's killing domestic opponents to advance an ideology, and collateral deaths during wartime. However, Dave's attempts to drag in the U.S. government is a familiar left-wing tactic. I therefore shifted the conversation back to Antifa, because even if we concede for the sake of argument that the United States government commits terrorist acts, that still does not answer the question of whether Antifa engages in similar acts, albeit to a lesser degree. Again, left-wing thinkers simply want to deflect the argument and say Antifa is not "as bad," when compared to other groups. Even if that were true, Antifa is still a terrorist group.

In the end, Dave did make a plea that I took to heart. He told me that he had never engaged in any violent behavior, so it was "scary" to have me and the other students call him a terrorist, and alluded to the Red Scare of the '50s.

The Red Scare was a time when sympathizing with socialism or communism, or supporting other people's right to believe in these ideas, led to being shunned, fired, or demonized. It was a dark time in American history. No one should be persecuted for merely believing in a hateful ideology, no matter how wrong or dangerous one may believe it to be. We should convince people to abandon hateful ideologies, not imprison or hurt them for having different opinions.

Dave argued that my call to designate Antifa as a terrorist organization encouraged people to fear socialists and communists. One should prosecute Antifa activists who engage in acts of political violence only. Nonetheless, if one does not actually commit political violence, it does not mean they should get off scot-free. In criminal law, an accomplice or principal in the second degree may be convicted of the crimes of the principal if it can be proven that they intentionally and knowingly assisted in the commission of the crime. At the very least, every person who engages in the black bloc provides cover for those who participate in violent acts. So while they are not the ones throwing the punches, many Antifa activists would still deserve the terrorist designation under accomplice liability.

This theory is expressed by several states' penal codes, in the form of gang affiliation statutes. The California Penal Code Section 186.22(a) makes it a crime to actively participate in a group, knowing that its members engage in criminal activity, and criminalizes promoting or assisting the criminal conduct of other gang members.[11] Like the terrorist acts statute defined above, Antifa also meets this definition. People who join Antifa, though they may never engage in political violence, actively assist in the criminal conduct of political violence. Declaring Antifa a terrorist organization would not be to criminalize radical left-wing politics. It would criminalize only the act of aiding and abetting those who commit political violence. The terrorist label would merely give the federal government the same power state governments already have to fight other types of criminal enterprises.

After an ardent conversation on Antifa's domestic terrorism, the conversation turned to the differences between capitalism and socialism. Every student in the club joined the discussion. Dave explained that he was a grad student in the school's economics department, which boasts a left-wing orientation, and I think it is worth highlighting some of the ideas he shared.

First, he told us that there was no difference, at least in his mind, between socialism and communism. While politicians like Senator Bernie Sanders wish to make a distinction, many left-wing thinkers and grassroots activists see socialism as a precursor to communism. Dave did, however, argue that his vision for society was to get rid of government. In effect, he was calling for an anarcho-collectivist society.

When we pressed him on how goods should be allocated, he proposed a system in which corporations democratically elected leaders who would then decide who should get what. He claimed that this was not a government. Yet his ideas were still a form of central planning. I posed several questions to him about this concept. What if I do not want to be part of this economy? Am I allowed to leave? In more words than one, he said no. That is not what I would call an absence of government. Yet Dave and other so-called "democratic" socialists do not see the irony in their logic. Democracy sounds good, but as the founders believed, democratic societies often lead to the tyranny of the majority.

Dave also rejected the "propaganda" that Cubans fled the communist dictatorship of Fidel Castro. He refused to acknowledge, that for decades people fled Cuba for America by every conceivable means. He also proclaimed that Cuba was not actually communist. According to him, these arguments were made by the U.S. government to delegitimize radical ideologies like his.

Communism and socialism often sound attractive to people because they propose to care for those who cannot work or who are struggling to get by. In 2019, a poll showed 43 percent of Americans believed socialism was good for the country.[12] Yet I believe the reason younger people support socialism is because they are not old enough to remember its failures and crimes. Similarly, a 2020 poll showed that more than 15 percent of Italians do not believe in the Holocaust, which is up dramatically from 2.7 percent in 2004.[13] The reason history repeats itself is that normal people forget the sins of our past.

True to the antifascist socialist tradition, Dave also incorrectly argued that capitalism is either a precursor or synonymous with fascism. And therein lies the truth about Antifa. When Antifa says it is fighting fascism, it really means capitalism.

While Dave certainly gave an impassioned defense of antifascist activism, his critiques of capitalism were not well-founded. Antifa members are not the defenders of the poor and defenseless. They have an agenda to destroy anything that does not align with their Far-Left socialist views, and are willing to use violence to achieve their faux-utopian society.

For better or worse, socialism should be debated on the public stage. It is only when Antifa members cross the line from philosophy to violence that they should be prosecuted under domestic terrorist statutes. To declare Antifa a terrorist organization is not to punish its anticapitalistic propaganda, but to punish the members for the political violence in which they often engage. The recent wave of violence in the summer of 2020, in cities across America, has made this violent propensity impossible to ignore.

CHAPTER 7

IN DEFENSE OF FREE SPEECH

For most of this book, I detailed the problem that is Antifa. Through my own eyes, I have unmasked what fuels it and explained why it is a terrorist organization that should be fought tooth and nail with every legal means possible. No rational person should ever consider Antifa other than a net negative for society. However, it is also essential to recognize its stated purpose. Antifa's mission appears to be a noble one. It seeks to rid the world of fascism, a dangerous philosophy that has led to the demise of millions of people.

Mark Bray's *Antifascist Handbook* tells stories of Jewish people who are beaten and terrorized, and portrays Antifa as protectors of the Jewish faith. The same goes for other minorities who are indeed under attack. In each instance, Bray gives examples in which Antifa's militant tactics appear to be warranted. Bray's problem, however, is that he conflates the issues. He believes that Antifa can destroy fascism, or at least keep it at bay. But it cannot. Fascism is an ideology that will forever be embraced by some malignant individuals. Antifa cannot destroy fascism any more than I can destroy socialism and communism, which have murdered millions more people than fascism.

People will always hold dangerous ideas, but sometimes attacking them head-on only increases their popularity. Antifa is not the protector of anyone but its own failed ideology.

In this chapter, it is worth exploring the free speech debate. I do this to weigh in against honest liberals who despise Antifa, but have a mistaken belief that hate can be eliminated through legislation. These liberals honestly believe that hatred can be removed or disempowered by banning hateful speech. In my opinion, hate speech legislation is not useful, and it would backfire and be a net negative for society.

Many people wonder about the difference between hate speech and free speech. However, the false dichotomy suggests two things. First, that the government can ban hate speech because it is different in kind from free speech. And second, it forces free speech advocates to proclaim, "Hate speech is free speech," which is not a good look. To equate both types of speech allows anti-free-speech advocates to decry free speech altogether, as it appears to serve no positive function in society.

If free speech is just hate speech, why protect it? However, hate speech is just like any other type of speech. Thus, there are two better questions to pose. The first is, *What is hate speech?* Once hate speech is defined, then honest philosophers can ask, *Should hate speech receive First Amendment protections?*

For an authoritative definition of hate speech, one can look to the United Nations. According to one of its reports, hate speech is "any kind of communication in speech, writing or behaviour that attacks or uses pejorative or discriminatory language with reference to a person or a group on the basis of who they are, in other words, based on their religion, ethnicity, nationality, race, colour, descent, gender or other identity factor."[1] The classic case against hate speech is simple and clear-cut. Liberal advocates target egregious forms of expression that discriminate against a person as described above.

Now comes the second question: Should speech like that be allowed in a decent society?

Many liberals will answer in the negative and propose hate speech bans. A significant defense of hate speech legislation comes from Professor Jeremy Waldron of NYU Law School. Waldron believes hate speech laws would protect minority communities, and argues that "each person, each member of each group, should be able to go about his or her business, with the assurance that there will be no need to face hostility, violence, discrimination, or exclusion by others."[2] In a perfect society, people should not have to face hostility while engaging in peaceful acts. Yet while we should always strive for a better society, hate speech legislation does not appear to improve the safety of individuals.

For example, the United Kingdom and Canada have strict hate speech laws, yet America still has fewer violent hate crimes. According to the Office for Democratic Institutions and Human Rights, the United States had 7,699 hate crimes in 2010, with a population of about 309.3 million people.[3] Just north of the border, Canada had a total of 1,401 hate crimes with a population of 34.1 million residents.[4] While there were fewer hate crimes in Canada overall, Canada still had more hate crimes per capita. Not to mention the United Kingdom, which registered a staggering 48,127 hate crimes, excluding Scotland, with a population of 62.77 million people.[5]

Now, granted, if hate groups have the freedom to speak, they still may incite violence. But speech likely to incite violence is already banned in America. Moreover, having hate groups out in the open has a significant benefit in that it makes them visible to the public. Their visibility allows the government to monitor and thwart any plans they may have to cause violence. Leftists and liberal students who propose hate speech laws say they want them because they believe they will protect human dignity. However, there is more dignity in walking away from an insult with one's head up than in being a victim of violence. Defending all speech will make it easier to maintain peace, and thus, preserve civility.

Liberals may object to such reasoning, claiming that American history is replete with hate crimes, even without hate speech bans, such as in the post-Civil War South. These types of events are often used as justifications for the creation of hate speech laws in the first place. However, hate crimes in the South were not due to the lack of hate speech laws. They were a complex issue of their time, and had many causes. The Fourteenth Amendment prevents states from denying "to any person within its jurisdiction the equal protection of the laws."[6] State officials in the South ignored this provision. They refused to prosecute crimes against blacks because the officials themselves perpetuated many of the crimes, and they could not be thrown out of office, because they concealed their identities.

While censorship has little direct effect on curbing hate group activity with regards to violent crime, there are other consequences that censorship advocates directly influence. Because of censorship advocates, some now argue that if an expression causes emotional distress to another, the speech should be banned. While Waldron would likely disagree and propose bans of only egregious speech, the consequences of his argument have led college campuses in the direction of almost total censorship. For example, the University of New Hampshire (UNH) published a list of words it considered problematic.[7] The list included terms such as American, elders, senior citizens, overweight, speech impediment, dumb, sexual preference, manpower, freshmen, mailman, and chairman. After the story broke, the university received negative national attention, prompting the President, Mark W. Huddleston, to release this statement:

> While individuals on our campus have every right to express themselves, I want to make it absolutely clear that the views expressed in this guide are NOT the policy of the University of New Hampshire. I am troubled by many things in the language guide, especially the suggestion that the use of the term "American" is misplaced or offensive. The only UNH policy on speech is that it is free and unfettered on our campuses. It is ironic that what was probably a well-meaning effort to be "sensitive" proves offensive to many people, myself included.

Huddleston's last sentence is the most significant line. Hate speech bans were meant to protect people from offensive material, but in turn create a society in which people are offended by innocuous language.

This also explains why modern Antifa does not fight only actual fascists, but anyone with whom they disagree. As Mark Bray says, Antifa is also there to fight against "everyday fascists." The consequences of hate speech bans have led Antifa to perceive everything to be offensive and everything to be a form of oppression. Advocates for hate speech bans have made it so Antifa will never run out of targets.

The University of New Hampshire case is not an isolated event. There is a trend of college campuses using censorship in the hope of protecting the mental health of young adults. While at first glance this seems a worthwhile goal, its effects are counterproductive. According to authors Greg Lukianoff and Jonathan Haidt, censorship harms the well-being of students.[8] In their *Atlantic* magazine article, "The Coddling of the American Mind," the authors highlight a basic psychological principle: "According to the most basic tenets of psychology, helping people with anxiety disorders avoid the things they fear is misguided."

The emotional well-being component can be traced to arguments like Waldron's human dignity argument. His reasoning has now spread to college campuses throughout America, and is currently hindering the free exchange of ideas, a basic tenet of American society.

Lukianoff and Haidt's article has several examples of demands for censorship from both academic and social interactions. One of the most striking attempts at suppressing speech is a case from Harvard Law School, in which law students asked the school "not to teach rape law—or, in one case, even use the word violate (as in 'that violates the law')." Proponents of this type of censorship are no longer calling it outright hate speech, instead referring to it as *microaggressions*.

A microaggression is a form of subtle discrimination, even if the person responsible had no intent to offend. While the term is different, the solution has the same result: banning speech. One example given by Lukianoff and Haidt is that "by some campus guidelines, it is a microaggression to ask an Asian American or Latino American, 'Where were you born?,' because this implies that he or she is not a real American"[9] And this is the general problem with Waldron's argument. Following his argument in defense of human dignity does little to protect humanity, but rather violates the dignity of democracy and debate.

Colleges, by design, are supposed to be bastions of discussion and free thought. However, the arguments for censorship in defense of human dignity have backfired. Now, students are defying the basic tenet of free thought and debate when they refuse to have frank conversations because the subjects may be troubling.

Commenting on the Lukianoff-Haidt article, former President Barack Obama said, "I don't agree that you, when you become students at colleges, have to be coddled and protected from different points of view.[10] Obama continued, "Anybody who comes to speak to you and you disagree with, you should have an argument with them. But you shouldn't silence them by saying, 'You can't come because, you know, my—I'm too sensitive to hear what you have to say.' That is not the way we learn either."

Yet while colleges are supposed to create an environment of intellectual diversity, many college students have become proponents of banning basic vocabulary.

A society that begins by banning words will end by banning books, and ideas themselves. Indeed, book bans are no longer a concept found only in science fiction novels like Ray Bradbury's *Fahrenheit 451*. In June 2015, Lou Lumenick, a prominent movie critic, called for a government-enforced ban on *Gone with the Wind*. As reported by The Guardian, "'[t]he book, as well as the film,' says Lumenick, 'buys heavily into the idea that the Civil War was a noble lost cause and casts Yankees and Yankee sympathisers [sic] as the villains.'"[11]

A government that bans books that pose no conceivable imminent danger is inherently more oppressive than a society that allows hate speech. If a hate group attacks someone, the victim can call the police. If the state arrests someone for possessing a book that it considers undeserving of protection, there is no one left to call.

A society that bans hate speech will eventually ban basic vocabulary and controversial, yet relevant, literature that seeks to stimulate discussions necessary for the health of American culture. Censorship of speech that poses no imminent danger categorically departs from American values. However, free speech does come at a cost. People often abuse their freedoms, and free speech is no exception. However, the societal consequences of banning hate speech are more harmful than the perceived benefits.

As President Obama said at the 2012 United Nations General Assembly, "Efforts to restrict speech can become a tool to silence critics or repress minorities….the strongest weapon against hateful speech is not repression: it is more speech—the voices of tolerance that rally against bigotry and blasphemy, and lift up the values of understanding and mutual respect."[12]

Ultimately, hate speech deserves First Amendment protection because the alternative would put us on a path toward tyranny.

Legal Ramifications

Although liberals want to ban hate speech, the First Amendment prevents them from doing so. Therefore, if hate speech law proponents wanted to change American law, they must amend the Constitution. However, banning speech would not only affect one's ability to say what one wants. It would also have a wide-ranging effect on the legal standard for defamation. In tort law, defamation is a published false and defamatory statement about another person that causes the victim damages. Although our defamation statute traces its roots to English common law, the torts are treated differently in American and English jurisdictions. One significant difference is that the English common law dealt with defamation as a tort of strict liability. This means that once the elements of the law are met, the defendant is liable and has to pay damages, no matter if the statement at issue was true. The First Amendment worries that strict liability would have a chilling effect on freedom of speech. Thus, truth is always a complete defense in defamation suits. However, the First Amendment does much more than remove strict liability. It may sometimes protect false statements. As Justice William Brennan wrote in *NAACP v. Button* (1963), "Because First Amendment freedoms need breathing space to survive, government may regulate in the area only with narrow specificity."[13] For legitimate speech to thrive, the First Amendment must sometimes protect speech that is false and disliked.

Speech about a public figure is far more protected. For a public figure to succeed in a defamation suit, the plaintiff must establish that the publisher had "actual malice," a term of art coined in *New York Times Co. v. Sullivan* (1964), which means that the defamatory comment was made "with knowledge that it was false or with reckless disregard of whether it was false or not."[14] Thus it is not enough to prove falsity. It is also necessary to prove that the defendant knew the statements were false or acted recklessly, whether they were true or not. The reason for this is simple: the First Amendment needs breathing room. Americans need to be free to discuss subjects of public controversy without fear of politicians litigating newspapers and critics into silence.

Another attempt to pierce the First Amendment was made in 1988 in *Hustler Magazine v. Falwell*.[15] In this suit, a famous conservative preacher was defamed through a satirical advertisement.

The parody suggested he had an incestuous relationship with his mother, and that he lectured intoxicated at all his sermons. A court threw out the defamation, claim but allowed a tort of intentional infliction of emotional distress to go to a jury. That tort occurs when a person intentionally causes the victim to suffer severe emotional distress because of the extreme and outrageous behavior of the defendant. A jury found that the false allegations were extreme and outrageous, and awarded the plaintiff $200,000 in actual and punitive damages.

The Supreme Court overruled the award and afforded First Amendment rights to parodies, no matter if they are extreme and outrageous. While the intentional infliction of emotional distress was dismissed as a "novel question," and the Court reaffirmed the First Amendment, that novel argument has gained a lot of support in recent years. Such support is mainly found among liberal and leftist college students.

According to a 2019 study commissioned by the Knight Foundation, 41 percent of college students in America believe the First Amendment should not protect hate speech.[16] This statistic is troubling because colleges are laboratories for future American policy. Not only are there many supporters of hate speech bans on college campuses, but many students have already put these egregious speech bans into practice.

At UC Irvine, the student government wrote legislation to change the student code of conduct regarding slander and libel. According to their code, slander and libel are respectively defined as speech or writing purveyed "with the intent of upsetting another person."[17] If a constitutional amendment were adopted based on the language preferred by college students, the truth would no longer be a defense against defamation. The new standard would be the old strict liability standard, but worse. Under strict liability, at least one had to prove damages to reputation or business. Under this new standard, the injuries are simply emotional. This would dramatically lower the threshold for the tort of intentional infliction of emotional distress. Under that tort, the defendant's behavior must be extreme and outrageous. To cite an earlier example, using the word *American* would be enough to sue for damages under either tort.

If a hate speech exception like those proposed by students had existed during the *Hustler* case, the plaintiff would have won because the tort would be that the plaintiff suffered emotional distress. This ruling would have killed parody, even if the subject was an elected official. The first effect of hate speech constitutional amendments would therefore be the death of entertainment. There would be no *Simpsons*, *Saturday Night Live*, or *Onion*, nor would there be cartoon caricatures in the Sunday paper. If a plaintiff can allege that such depictions made them severely emotionally distraught, or merely upset or uncomfortable, they could silence entertainment. But that is not the only issue. Overturning *Hustler* would also result in the death of legitimate criticisms of public figures.

Since the controlling element under a hate speech amendment would be the emotional harm to the plaintiff, politicians would take advantage of the situation. There would be no more breathing room for legitimate criticisms. For example, President Trump could call foul when a blimp made to look like a baby Trump flies over his home. Senators and congressmen would sue for emotional damages every time the media took a swipe at them. An article questioning people's religious beliefs in relation to their morality as elected officials would be actionable.

Take the time Speaker Nancy Pelosi shot back at a reporter who asked if she hated President Trump. Pelosi claimed that she does not hate anyone, because she is Catholic.[18] You could hear her anger and disdain. Since the controlling element in a defamation case would be the emotional harm suffered by the plaintiff, Speaker Pelosi would be able to sue the reporter, claiming offense as her primary argument to shut down his legitimate question.

The adoption of hate speech doctrines in American jurisprudence would return defamation law into the old saying, *The greater the truth, the greater the libel.*

CHAPTER 8

BRIDGING OUR POLITICAL DIVIDE

If my dad taught me to fight with passion, my mom taught me how to fight smart.

It is a tragedy that children do not listen to their parents' advice until they are grown. I know now that if I had listened to my mom's advice, I would have avoided tons of trouble throughout my life.

For example, when I was nineteen, I was arrested after leaving my then girlfriend's birthday party. She lived in Pomona, and it normally took me ten to fifteen minutes to get home to Azusa. Before I left, she told me to be careful and take the freeway, but for some reason I wanted to take the streets. While on a main street, I went through a DUI checkpoint and found myself in handcuffs within thirty seconds of talking to an officer.

Now, to be clear, I do not drink, nor do I do drugs. I remember seeing kids as young as thirteen and fourteen getting drunk and high with a variety of concoctions. From forty-ounce beers and hard alcohol to marijuana, NOS gas, and cocaine, it is easy for children to get hold of drugs and narcotics. Yet from ages sixteen to eighteen, I used to spend time on the weekend and after school at a home we called the crust pad. It really should have been called the crack house because it was full of drugs and squatters. I do not like to remember my time inside this house. However, the only time I have ever done drugs was the time a "friend" unknowingly drugged me in high school.

Yet the night I was arrested, I was under the influence of my own ego. First, I was in my first serious relationship, which made me feel invincible. Plus, I had recently won a student government election by a two-to-one margin. Additionally, I was accepted into a couple of honor societies and had a new job, which was not in a warehouse or in retail. My life seemed to be going exactly as planned. I thought I could take on the world with words.

On top of that, I had recently watched countless videos of DUI checkpoints in which civil libertarians stood up for their Fourth Amendment rights. In these videos, the drivers refused to show their licenses until the officers provided their probable cause to stop them. Of course, my mom had previously told me not to be stupid and comply if I ever found myself in such a situation. But I was high on a self-righteous ego. Ironically, I had a box of U.S. pocket Constitutions in my backseat, given to me by the Leadership Institute. I was foolish enough to believe I could assert my Fourth Amendment rights and be let go.

If you want to make God laugh, tell him your plans.

As I approached, I saw some orange cones, followed by several officers who directed me to a complete stop. As I waited, the blue and red lights blinded me, making my chest tighten. I knew what I was going to do. I had planned and prepared for that moment for weeks. I began to think of the perfect line to make the officer understand that what he was doing was unconstitutional and a violation of my Fourth Amendment rights.

As I pulled near the officer, he told me to lower my window, and I said I could not do that. But before I could finish the sentence, he reached for the door handle and told me I was under arrest. I had gotten away with so much as a kid. Yet the one time I thought I was right on the law, I was going to jail.

What followed was an uncomfortable thirty-six hours. It was the weekend, so I was held for longer than I would have been otherwise. At first, I was put in a cell with someone who was around my age. But after they transferred him, they brought in a drunk and I began to fear for my safety. I could hardly sleep as I heard him snoring in the bunk below mine. The next day, they put me in a holding cell with about twenty to thirty detainees. Some had been stopped for DUI offenses, and others for gang-related crimes. That's when I realized I was no longer a kid before the law. I realized my actions had consequences.

I was charged with failure to obey a peace officer, a misdemeanor in California. Not the worst offense, but it was overreaching. I should have been charged with failure to furnish identification to a peace officer, which is a mere infraction. To this day, I believe the Supreme Court erred on this issue. The Court should have found sobriety checkpoints to be mere fishing expeditions that violate the Fourth Amendment. Yet none of that mattered that night. Had I listened to my mom and given the officer my ID, I would have been home in ten minutes. But due to my inflated ego, I was late to my first day of work as a math tutor, and had my family and friends worried sick.

The lesson I learned here was not, *Accept authority without question*, but *Pick your battles*. As any attorney will say, comply with an officer first, and then fight him in court.

Often, our self-righteous egos blind us. We act on impulse; we act based on emotions.

I consider the night I was arrested the first of two momentous experiences that helped me grow from an immature child into a thoughtful adult. The second came four months later, after my breakup, where again I acted on impulse instead of reason. Sometimes it takes pain and suffering to grow up. It is important to be passionate. Some causes are worth fighting for. But at the same time, one must grapple with reality and consider one's actions. Acting purely on emotions is dangerous.

This is the problem with Antifa members. Their passion for equality and fairness, and their self-righteous ideology, overshadows their reasoning and moral character. They are blind to their actions and their consequences. They fail to understand that beating up a reporter does not quash fascism. If Andy Ngo was truly a fascist, Antifa only helped promote his ideology; thousands of people now support him.

Antifa activists believe in the fairy tale that with enough punches and organized attacks, they can beat fascism into submission. However, as Newton's Third Law of Motion states, "For every action, there is an equal and opposite reaction." For every person Antifa beats up, innocent or not, there is a growing reaction against them. Violence against peaceful people creates nonpeaceful people. And if they were not peaceful to begin with, then expect escalation.

There has got to be a better way to deal with people in politics, and life in general.

Luckily, there is.

For several years, I have traveled the country visiting conservative students in lions' dens—college campuses. I have visited almost every major school in California, including the entire University of California system, the California State University system, as well as private colleges like Stanford, Santa Clara University, the University of Southern California, and the Claremont Colleges. In each school, I have found conservative or libertarian students who tell me strikingly similar stories of liberal bias and abuse.

But I not only help these students, I often work with other conservative activists who promote similar efforts, either as paid activists or volunteers. Just as I learned leftist tactics from various anarchists who came before me, I have learned a variety of strategies for engaging the Left, from numerous conservative and libertarian activists. Their strategies are not only peaceful, but more effective.

When I was a field representative for the Leadership Institute, I answered a call from a reporter at Campus Reform who had just received an email from a concerned student who witnessed leftist activists harass and disrupt a pro-life display on their college campus. The email claimed that the University Women's Resource and Research Center supported the agitators, who were mostly left-wing students. The pro-life students were new activists, so they were scared and did not know what to do about the organized opposition they encountered. While all the reporter wanted to know was whether I knew someone on campus so she could quote for her story, I knew that I needed to act.

While I had an extensive network of conservative students, many attacks do not garner the publicity they deserve because many of the victims we help do not document these incidents. If that student had not sent an email, we at the Leadership Institute might have never heard about it, and the administration would have gone further to suppress the rights of the pro-life students.

It was around 9:15 p.m. that night when I told the Campus Reform reporter, "Don't worry, I'll be there." I had a few things to do before I left—mostly the errands I had promised my mom. I also visited my girlfriend (now my wife). Eventually, around 11:00 p.m., I began my seven-hour journey to UC Davis.

As I was driving, I listened to podcasts, music, and other material. My car always seemed to be a mess, full of junk food, water bottles, clipboards, pens, markers, flyers, posters, stickers, and usually a folding table—everything we needed for an impromptu activism project. My coworkers and I would compete to see who had the record for most miles driven. I drove almost forty thousand miles in one year alone, for the conservative movement. If I added up all the miles I have driven for the conservative cause, it would be roughly half the distance to the moon.

At around 5:00 or 6:00 a.m., I stopped at a gas station to take a nap. I have not only seen countless colleges and universities, I have also seen a lot of Wal-Mart parking lots and gas station rest stops. When people ask me where I lived in Colorado, I joke about having different homes throughout the state. In fact, I had a comfortable pillow and blankets in my backseat, which took me to different dark alleys and parking lots. My favorite place to stop was in the parking lot of a Planet Fitness in Loveland, Colorado, where I spent many freezing nights. I chose this place because the gym was open twenty-four hours, so my car blended in with the rest.

After an hour nap at the gas station, I awoke and began my last stretch. Since I had never been to UC Davis, I parked far away and got lost. It is a huge campus. Eventually, I found the main quad, where everyone sets up a table to recruit students. It was slow at first, but I soon met some activists who were setting up a project. Their display said, "Do you think abortion should be allowed?" People could come up and write their names under a banner that said "Yes, No, Maybe." It seemed harmless enough and not remotely controversial. I began to wonder if the report I had heard was incorrect and my trip had been a wasted effort.

Ultimately, the leftist cavalry was summoned. Dozens of student activists, some advised by what appeared to be faculty or university staff, began to gather around us. Some were shouting insults, while others only held signs. At first, I was a quiet observer—nothing egregiously wrong with what they were doing. These students were merely exercising their First Amendment rights. It may have been distasteful with the insults they hurled, but the First Amendment must protect all speech, even theirs. Liberal students have every right to gather and organize against conservatives as long as their speech does not escalate into censorship or, as it is commonly known, the heckler's veto.

I began to get involved when I noticed the leftist activists were accosting passing students who were interested in the pro-life display. The cavalry created a human shield to prevent people from engaging with the pro-life students, and routinely interrupted peaceful conversations with club officers.

As I explained earlier, this is the culture of UC Davis left-wing students. I have been on this campus about six times since that incident, and experienced similar resistance.

After several disruptions, some students called the campus police to prevent the situation from escalating. The police created space between the opposing groups, and warned the leftist activists not to disturb our free speech rights.

Their group began to grow in numbers and signs, and its people even brought balloons. That is when my inner activist kicked in. I went to the store and bought a dozen poster boards to make "birthday signs." After all, the counter-protesters appeared to be hosting a birthday party that celebrated life and the pro-life movement. That angered a few of them, until eventually one of the activists threw the group's tabling materials to the ground. Again, this is how their mentality works. If their "nonviolent" means are not successful, they are willing to escalate to disruption, and ultimately violence. Luckily, a police officer who witnessed the incident detained and questioned her. I remember seeing what appeared to be a university staff member help her avoid arrest by mediating her conversation with the officer.

I took pictures of the activism project from different angles. I guess this act was not well received, because a student ran toward me, got in my face, and shouted for me to stop. He was irate that I had taken pictures of the activists "without consent." I said I had a right to do so because there was no expectation of privacy in the public space, but this only made him angrier, so I attempted to de-escalate the situation. My attempts, however, were proving to be futile. He started yelling louder, inching toward my face while making thinly veiled threats. Luckily, another activist, an older gentleman, stepped in and made sure the situation did not turn ugly. After he pulled me away, he told me that they had had problems with that student in the past, and that I should stay away from him.

This experience was no different from other activism projects I have helped with. My coworkers and I routinely share stories about how our students are assaulted, our tables flipped, and many other altercations. Hayden Williams is not the first conservative activist to be attacked by leftist thugs, and unfortunately, he has not been the last. There is, however, a significant distinction between those incidents and this one.

One of the people I met that day was named Josh Brahm. Josh is the founder of the Equal Rights Institute, and he is a pro-life apologist and philosopher. I have never heard a better pro-life speaker. Josh Brahm has a fabulous pro-life argument that he calls the equal rights argument. He believes in equal rights for adults, children, and unborn babies. In truth, I am simplifying his case. But the key takeaway is not the content of his argument, but his demeanor. Josh does not appear to be a confrontational guy. However, I have seen him perform in debates and deliver passionate speeches. However, he knows how not to allow his passion to drive him. Instead, he uses it as fuel.

While on the quad, I looked toward Josh and was surprised to see him already in action. There were about a dozen liberal college students, all female, surrounding him. Some had previously approached the table aggressively, ready to give everyone a piece of their minds. Yet instead of retreating or calling for help, Josh was sitting on the table with his legs crossed, relaxed, just talking to these women. He did not shout. He did not call them ugly names. He did not cast blame upon them. Instead, he listened to their concerns and addressed each of them individually.

But he did more than that. He did not just listen to respond, he listened to understand. Before answering, Josh takes the time to restate their argument, and sometimes strengthen their case. He does this to make sure the people he talks to feel comfortable sharing their ideas, and in turn, they are receptive of his statements. As Josh says, "Some pro-choice people will not change their mind after one conversation on a college campus. Some of them will only change their mind after dozens of conversations with a person they trust, in the context of friendship."[1]

Josh listens before speaking. And when he is responding, he does not merely state his beliefs. He makes sure they understand him, not in debate, but in the way a friend talks to another friend. There is a time and place for activism, and a time and place for dialogue. While I was busy holding people accountable, Josh was changing hearts and minds. Don't get me wrong—we need activism. The advocacy that my colleagues and I promote is incredibly important. When student rights are being violated every week, the conservative movement needs to vigorously defend our constitutional liberties. Conservative activism requires one to be courageous and fearless in the face of leftist thugs and willing to punch back when necessary. But at the same time, we must remember that our political opponents are not our enemies; they are just people.

Antifa works by dehumanizing others, picking a target, freezing it, and polarizing it to destroy it. This tactic can be effective, but it can also be harmful to human relations. It is natural for one to want to be a courageous liberator—the defender of the weak and helpless. However, members of Antifa allow their self-righteous mentality to overpower them, so they lash out against those with whom they disagree.

To those who may believe such interactions are no longer possible in mainstream politics, I offer the relationship that Republican Congressman Trey Gowdy and Democratic Congressman Elijah Cummings shared while they were in Congress. Sadly, upon Congressman Cummings's death, many people hatefully rejoiced. Yet conservative hero Gowdy lamented his death and invoked the mutual respect the Far-Left Democrats and he had once shared:

"We tried to understand where the other had come from, what made us who we were, why we believed what we believed."[2] Their mutual respect of one another as political adversaries is what we should be striving for in modern political discourse.

Josh Brahm likes to say that he is 98 percent sure that what he is doing is absolutely right. Such a practice keeps him humble. But it also keeps him sharp. Because when one admits that there is a possibility of being incorrect, one begins to approach a conversation with caution and in search of the truth, not merely to prove another person wrong. This practice leads one to accept challenging questions to one's ideology. To deal with it. To struggle with it. To come to terms with it. And in the end, it makes one a better advocate.

On the other hand, it is OK to admit you are wrong.

I admitted to being wrong while in Antifa. To this day, I am about 97 percent sure I am doing the right thing. I am 99 percent sure there is a God. I am 98 percent sure Conservatism is the best philosophy for the future of America. In the end, I do not like to deal in absolutes, because life is messy and unpredictable. We must be flexible and allow for change, unless we want to go down the rabbit hole of self-righteous hatred.

I was not even eighteen when I did all these things. I wish I could go back and apologize to that CEO. I wish I would have listened and learned more about the issue before disturbing his neighbors and his home. I did not know his name, yet I made him my enemy. I wish I could apologize to that business owner and repay the damages I caused, but I do not know which McDonalds I targeted. I am glad that I never physically hurt anyone, because that would torment me for the rest of my life.

The only way I know how to make amends is to pay it forward. I am thankful that our society looks at the person you are today, and not at the mistakes of your past. Coming to America is likely the best decision my parents could have made. In Mexico, there was no future for me, and thanks to them, I am now doing my best to live happy, live free, and help students so they do not have to live in fear of leftist attacks.

Today, I help students defend themselves against Antifa because I know exactly how they operate. But I also want to be the same person that Adam once was to me. The person who helps anyone who wants to come out of Antifa or abandon leftist ideology and avoid the mistakes I once made. I also want to be the person Josh Brahm was to these liberal pro-choice women. One who looks for friendship before looking for problems.

There is a common joke about first-year students who think they know everything about human behavior simply because they have taken Psych 101. I feel like that is what is happening with American colleges. As my mom once told me, some people become so smart that they start acting dumb.

Every person reading this book has one thing in common: we are all human. We get angry, we fight, we love, we make mistakes. I know I made a lot.

But please do not let denying others their right to speak be your mistake.

I am often asked if I believe that political violence is ever justified. I usually respond that it never is. Still, I think the issue is more complicated than a mere platitude. One could call me a hypocrite for taking such a stand because I believe in the cause of liberty. But I also condemn left-wing activists who spout violence. Some may say I do not support Antifa merely because I do not agree with its politics. Yet it is not the black-or-white issue many assume. Political violence is a complex issue that has varying degrees of wrongfulness. Unfortunately, the mainstream media, activist professors, and many leftist students often demand a short answer that they can use to attack me. They are not interested in a debate or discussion. They seek political victory at all costs.

The United States was born because people wanted to fight tyranny. These same people later adopted the Second Amendment, which reads, "A well regulated militia being necessary to the security of a free state, the right of the people to keep and bear arms shall not be infringed."

The founders adopted the Second Amendment so citizens could live free from oppression and tyranny. Thus, there seems to be an implicit proposition in the American creed, which endorses using force for revolutionary purposes. While their reasoning appears to justify acts of political violence, it does not. The founders were under imminent threat of harm to their lives and liberties from a Crown thousands of miles away. They were not politically motivated. They just wanted to live their lives.

The Second Amendment is a tool for defense, not offense, and it is an option of last resort, not one to be used every time Congress passes a law, or the wrong president is elected.

While Antifa is a leftist organization, some people are surprised to learn that many of its members are strong proponents of the Second Amendment—a position typically ascribed to the Right. While I have changed my political positions radically in the past ten years, the one stance I have always held is that everyone should have the right to be armed. There are Antifa-affiliated groups that fit the stereotype of right-wing militias, like the Redneck Revolt, which has chapters in over thirty states.[3] Antifa, and conservatives alike, recognize that without guns, fascist and tyrannical governments can take over. However, there is a difference between Antifa and conservatives in general: Conservatives support the Second Amendment in case the government tries to infringe on our rights. Antifa activists support the right to bear arms because they want to impose their will on others.

Political violence is never justified. The right to bear arms exists for the dire possibility that the government may turn tyrannous and take away the rights of individuals. It exists for self-defense, not offense. If Antifa had its way, its members would use this right to gun down anyone they despise, just as socialist and communist revolutions have done throughout history.

Political violence is never justified unless there is an imminent threat against one's life or liberty. But in such a case, the violence is no longer political; it is self-defense.

Political violence is inherently an offensive tactic, not a defensive one. One might say that the Guardian Angels, who are organizing to combat anti-Jewish hatred in New York City, practice a form of political violence because they are combating anti-Semitism.[4] If they were going around and attacking people who made antisemitic jokes, that would be political violence. Organizing to combat imminent threats against Jewish people in New York is not political violence; it is self-defense.

The founders were justified in using force against the Crown because Great Britain deprived them of their rights and liberties, daily. If you spoke out, you would be branded a turncoat and be chastised and terrorized. The colonies were under a systematic oppression which failed to give Americans a means to redress their grievances by petitioning the Crown.

Thankfully, Modern America does not do that. We have a system for resolving our grievances peacefully. It may have flaws, and we should always strive for improvement, but at the same time, one must remember that there is no perfect system. Thus, we should not pretend that the flaws in our system warrant forceful dismantlement. Show me an imminent threat to life or liberty without a peaceful means to resolve the issue, and then I may be convinced that force is necessary.

Even so, just because force may be justified does not mean it is the best solution.

Sometimes systems are prejudicial to change, and they must be challenged. Antifa attacks people who dare to question its motives. Unfortunately, its activists often attack the wrong people. They go after other peaceful citizens instead of agents of an oppressive government.

Take the recent protests in Hong Kong. Some have been violent, and people have been beaten on the streets by the Communist regime. Yet the student activists are not fighting supporters of the Chinese Communist Party; they are fighting the government itself, which has committed acts of violence against innocent people.[5]

At first, the protests were political. Hong Kong citizens wanted to stop a bad piece of legislation. But once the state began attacking peaceful protesters, the activists were entitled to fight back. In that case, the threat of imminent violence by the state warrants force. However, until that moment comes to America, and the government wantonly attacks peaceful people, Americans should settle their disputes in the courts or through the democratic process, not by taking to the streets.

Throughout American history, there have indeed been instances in which force against the government was warranted.

Nevertheless, some activists refused to go the way of Antifa. If the system is broken, we need to reform it with nonviolence, as Dr. Martin Luther King did.

Jim Powell, now a Senior Fellow at Cato Institute, wrote the book *The Triumph of Liberty*, which includes an essay that everyone should read. The piece is titled, "Militant Nonviolence: A Biography of Martin Luther King, Jr."[6] In this short biography, Powell describes the type of civil disobedience in which King engaged. Dr. King opposed the government to protest detestable racist laws. He organized protests that the government unconstitutionally shut down. While the issue would go through the legal process, as Powell points out, Southern courts refused to take up the matter with haste in order to further impede Dr. King's movement. The government in the post-Civil War American South was an oppressive regime that refused to allow African Americans to redress their concerns. That is one of the closest points in American history that we came to outright fascism.

Throughout his political career, Dr. King faced imminent threats to his life and liberty. He is an admirable and despised political activist. Eventually, he was assassinated. However, even in the face of imminent danger, he never preached violence. Jim Powell highlights one of Dr. King's most potent lines on the subject, when in 1964, he won the Nobel Peace Prize:

> As you press on with justice, be sure to move with dignity and discipline using only the weapon of love…Always avoid violence. If you succumb to the temptation of using violence in your struggle, unborn generations will be the recipients of a long and desolate night of bitterness, and your chief legacy to the future will be an endless reign of meaningless chaos…

In your struggle for justice, let your oppressor know that you are not attempting to defeat or humiliate him...you are merely seeking justice for him as well as yourself.[7]

Dr. King had every right to call for revolution. He and his people were oppressed, persecuted, lynched, and murdered in the streets. These crimes were committed by both private citizens and the state. But King knew that bloodshed would only increase tensions and fail to solve the problem. He had the platform to instigate violence, but he believed that nonviolence gave rise to more permanent social change.

Antifa's ideology is deeply flawed. The answer to fighting racism and fascism is not violence, but friendship and understanding. Musician Daryl Davis is likely the best example of this idea. For more than thirty years, Davis, a Black man, has dedicated his life to befriending KKK members. In this pursuit, he has gotten over two hundred hateful people to abandon their KKK robes, just by talking. As Davis said in an interview:

It's when the talking ceases that the ground becomes fertile for violence. If you spend five minutes with your worst enemy—it doesn't have to be about race, it could be about anything...you will find that you both have something in common. As you build upon those commonalities, you're forming a relationship, and as you build about that relationship, you're forming a friendship. That's what would happen. I didn't convert anybody. They saw the light and converted themselves.[8]

Even if Antifa is justified in fighting fascists with force, it is only creating a reactionary culture that breeds more violence.

During one of my events at the College of Charleston, in South Carolina, I had the opportunity to witness this idea in action. The Turning Point USA chapter that had invited me there was deeply connected with the local Republican Party. The room was filled with a diverse group of people, from conservatives to liberals. At the front of the room was an older gentleman covered in MAGA gear. Meanwhile, in the back there was a young African-American girl who came to oppose me. Luckily, the liberals in the room stayed for my speech and asked some tough questions. In the end, each attendant took my message seriously: Treat people as people, and not political pawns. After the event, it was heartwarming to see the young African-American girl and the MAGA gentleman engage in a civil conversation.

When I was invited to speak at Texas State University in San Marcos, Texas, I had about thirty to forty people in attendance, and for some reason I was nervous. After I was done with my speech, I began the Q&A period. Some people challenged what I said, but overall I found support.

Then someone asked, "What type of advice do you have for us?"

Until that point, I was unaware of the ideological makeup of the audience. I thought every student, except two, was Right-leaning. But they informed me that students from several LGBT, cultural studies, and liberal clubs were there. I was ecstatic—my target audience has always been liberals. My advice to them was, "Go get pizza and have a party. Be friends with one another and enjoy life."

A more extreme example comes from Charlottesville, Virginia radio host Joe Thomas. During the Conservative Political Action Conference in 2020, I had the opportunity to be interviewed by Thomas. Before the interview, Elaine (his wife) and I spoke for a few minutes. She told me that Joe had gone to the Charlottesville riot in 2017 to cover the event, and was assaulted multiple times. Leftist activists threw urine and pepper-sprayed him simply because he was white. Elaine showed me a picture when Joe was about to be beaten by an Antifa agitator. Luckily, Hawk Newsome, a leader in the Brooklyn, New York chapter of Black Lives Matter, intervened. According to Elaine, Newsome put his hand on Joe's shoulder and said, "Not him. He is cool." Joe Thomas, a conservative radio host, was saved by Hawk Newsome, a radical left-wing activist.

The reason Hawk intervened was because he had previously met Joe at a different event. A few months earlier, Joe covered another conference for his radio show and interviewed people from both the Right and the Left. He took a special liking to Hawk, and they spoke for over an hour not about politics, but about their lives. They developed a kinship over one brief conversation. That was enough for Hawk to recognize Joe as a person, and not a political pawn. It was Joe's friendship with Hawk that saved him.

Many talking heads think the Left and Right are both beyond saving, and that our culture will simply become more polarized until it breaks apart. However, the best way to bridge the political divides and roll back the threat of Antifa is to do what we have been doing for thousands of years: Be friends first, and political adversaries second.

The best way to fight hate is simply to talk to one another, understand our "enemies," and try to make them our friends.

ENDNOTES

Introduction

1 "The Mass Line: What it is and How to Use It," Liberation Road, https://roadtolibera-tion.org/the-mass-line-what-it-is-and-how-to-use-it/.

2 "Conservative Media is Living in the Past as Unrest Subsides Across the US," CNN, August 28, 2020, https://lite.cnn.com/en/article/h_bbd56104a6fcc982954809d6c968c197.

3 Ian Miles Cheong, "Ilhan Omar's Daughter Shows Support on Twitter for Antifa Group Organizing Riots in Minneapolis," *The Post Millennial*, May 28, 2020, https://thepostmillennial.com/ilhan-omars-daughter-shows-support-for-antifa-group-organizing-riots-in-minneapolis.

4 Andy Ngo, @MrAndyNgo, Twitter, May 31, 2020, 11:26 a.m., https://twitter.com/MrAndyNgo/status/1267115281635131393.

5 Daniella Silva and Matteo Moschella, NBC News, June 11, 2020, https://www.nbcnews.com/news/us-news/seattle-protesters-set-autonomous-zone-after-police-evacu-ate-precinct-n1230151.

6 House Judiciary GOP, @JudiciaryGOP, Twitter, June 25, 2020, 2:12 p.m., https://twitter.com/judiciarygop/status/1276216650442964994?lang=en.

7 Yael Halon, "Black Conservative Journalist Stabbed in Portland Says Americans 'Need to Wake Up,' 'Start Exposing Antifa,'" Fox News, July 30, https://www.foxnews.com/media/black-conservative-journalist-stabbed-portland-antifa-terrorist

8 Liz George, "Federal Agents May be Permanently Blinded by Lasers Used During Port-land Riots," July 31, 2020, https://americanmilitarynews.com/2020/07/federal-agents-may-be-permanently-blinded-by-lasers-used-during-portland-riots/

9 Ryan W. Miller, "CHAZ, a 'no Cop Co-Op': Here's What Seattle's Capitol Hill Autonomous Zone Looks Like," *USA Today*, June 12, 2020, https://www.usatoday.com/story/news/nation/2020/06/12/seattle-protest-chaz-capitol-hill-autonomous-zone-police-free/3173968001/.

10 Ibid.

11 Hallie Golden, "Seattle: One Teen Killed and Another Injured in Shooting in Police-Free Zone," *The Guardian*, June 29, 2020, https://www.theguardian.com/us-news/2020/jun/29/chop-chaz-shooting-seattle-police-free-zone.

12 Mickey Penguin, "Flux Of Pink Indians–F.C.T.U.L.P.–Alternative Mixes–1984," Kill Your Pet Puppy, September 22, 2009, killyourpetpuppy.co.uk/news/flux-of-pink-indians-f-c-t-u-l-p-alternative-mixes-1984.

Chapter 1

1 "25Point Plan," The National Socialist Movement Corporation, nsm88.org/25points/25pontscomplete.pdf.

2 Frances Dinkelspiel, "Berkeley Teacher Yvette Felarca Arrested on Charges of Inciting a Riot," *Berkeleyside*, September 27, 2017, www.berkeleyside.com/2017/07/19/berkeley-middle-school-teacher-yvette-felarca-arrested-charges-inciting-riot.

3 Lynsi Burton, "WTO Riots in Seattle: 15 Years Ago," *Seattle Post-Intelligencer*, November 29, 2014, https://www.seattlepi.com/local/article/WTO-riots-in-Seattle-15-years-ago-5915088.php.

4 CBS News, @CBSnews, Twitter, June 2, 2020, 1:55 p.m., https://twitter.com/CBSNews/status/1267877443911778306

5 James F. Jarboe, "Before the House Resources Committee, Subcommittee on Forests and Forest Health," The Federal Bureau of Investigations, FBI, February 12, 2002, archives.fbi.gov/archives/news/testimony/the-threat-of-eco-terrorism.

6 Tony Shin, "Reward Offered After Men Spray Chemical on 100 Dealership Cars," NBC Los Angeles, August 1, 2018, www.nbclosangeles.com/news/reward-offered-after-men-spray-chemical-on-dealership-cars/176662/.

7 Alinsky, Saul D. *Rules for Radicals* (Vintage Books, division of Random House, Inc., New York, 1989), pp. 130–34.

8 Senator Harry Reid, "Senator Reid on Koch Brothers," C-Span, Apr 1, 2014, www.c-span.org/video/?318628-4%2Fsen-reids-comments-koch-brothers.

9 "Who Are the Biggest Donors?," OpenSecrets.org, November 27, 2017, www.opensecrets.org/overview/topindivs.php?cycle=2016.

10 Robert D. McFadden, "David Koch, Billionaire Who Fueled Right-Wing Movement, Dies at 79," The New York Times, Aug 23, 2019, www.nytimes.com/2019/08/23/us/david-koch-dead.html.

11 Shannon, Deric, Asimakopoulos, John, and Nocella II, Anthony J. *The Accumulation of Freedom: Writings on Anarchist Economics* (AK Press, Oakland, Edinburgh, Baltimore, 2012).

12 Ibid. p. 16

13 Ibid., *The Accumulation of Freedom.*

14 Edwards, Chris, *Downsizing the Federal Government* (Cato Institute, Washington, D.C., 2005).

15 Bastiat, Frederic. *The Law* (G.P. Putnam & Sons, 1874).

16 "Opinion: Conservative Voices Needed at LBCC," *Viking News*, December 3, 2081, https://lbccviking.com/2018/12/opinion-conservative-voices-needed-at-lbcc.

17 "Uzuegbunam v. Preczewski," Alliance Defending Freedom, July 10, 2020, centerfor-academicfreedom.org/cases/uzuegbunam-v-preczewski/.

18 Alexander Pease, "University Gets Legal Warning for Enforcing Speech Rules Against Conservatives But Not Socialists," May 28, 2019, https://www.thecollegefix.com/university-gets-legal-warning-for-enforcing-speech-rules-against-conservatives-but-not-socialists/.

19 "Citrus College: Speech Code Litigation," Foundation for Individual Rights in Education (FIRE), 2003, www.thefire.org/cases/citrus-college-speech-code-litigation/.

Chapter 2

1 "El Documental Que Cambio a México ¡De Panzazo!," Evo Noticias channel, YouTube, December 23, 2012, www.youtube.com/watch?v=jyqhMOqyFs0.

2 Cullen, Jim. *The American Dream: A Short History of an Idea That Shaped a Nation* (Oxford University Press, 2006).

3 "Hispanic Media in the Balance," Media Research Center, https://www.mrc.org/special-reports/hispanic-media-balance.

4 Gutiérrez, Ramón. "George W. Bush and Mexican Immigration Policy," *Revue Française D'Études Américaines* (Berlin, Vol. 113, Issue 3, 2007) pp. 70–76. Cairn.Info, November 20, 2007, https://www.cairn-int.info/journal-revue-francaise-d-etudes-americaines-2007-3-page-70.htm.

5 Shane Goldmacher and Michael Rothfeld, "Schwarzenegger Cuts $500 million More as He Signs Budget," *Los Angeles Times*, July 29, 2009, www.latimes.com/local/la-me-california-budget29-2009jul29-story.html.

6 Catherine E. Shoichet, "Court: School Was Within Its Rights to Ban U.S. Flag T-shirts on Cinco de Mayo," CNN, March 3, 2014, www.cnn.com/2014/02/27/justice/california-school-american-flag-shirts/index.html.

7 Univision Noticias channel, "El Mensaje de un Grupo de Niños a Donald Trump," YouTube, November 13, 2016, www.youtube.com/watch?v=8dTUmFWr1nU.

8 Brooke Seipel, "Linda Ronstadt: Trump Is 'like Hitler, and the Mexicans Are the New Jews,'" The Hill, December 31, 2019, thehill.com/homenews/media/476417-linda-ronstadt-trump-is-like-hitler-and-the-mexicans-are-the-new-jews.

9 Andrew Kreighbaum, "White House Executive Order Prods Colleges on Free Speech, Program-Level Data and Risk Sharing," *Inside Higher Ed*, March 22, 2019, www.insidehighered.com/news/2019/03/22/white-house-executive-order-prods-colleges-free-speech-program-level-data-and-risk.

10 "The Nobel Peace Prize for 2009," The Nobel Prize, October 9, 2009, www.nobelprize.org/prizes/peace/2009/press-release/.

Chapter 3

1 "Black Rose Society Anarchist Historical Tour," Los Angeles Indymedia, https://la.indymedia.org/calendar/event_display_detail.php?event_id=8747.

ENDNOTES

2 Bray, Mark. *Antifa: The Antifascist Handbook* (Melville House Publishing, New York, 2017) p. 19.

3 Brigitte Studer, "In Stalins Gefolgschaft: Moskau und die KPD 1928–1933 (review)," Research Gate, January 2009, https://www.researchgate.net/publication/236724939_In_Stalins_Gefolgschaft_Moskau_und_die_KPD_1928-1933_review.

4 Theodore Draper, "The Ghost of Social-Fascism," *Commentary Magazine*, February 1969, www.commentarymagazine.com/articles/theodore-draper/the-ghost-of-social-fascism/.

5 "Verfassungsschutzbericht 2018," Bundesministerium des Innern, https://www.verfassungsschutz.de/download/vsbericht-2018.pdf. I don't speak German, but I loosely translated this line: "(…) der Kampf gegen den Faschismus ist erst gewonnen, wenn das kapitalistische System zerschlagen und eine klassenlose Gesellschaft erreicht ist." (Homepage „Antifaschistischer Aufbau München").

6 "Davies, Norman. *No Simple Victory: World War II in Europe, 1939-1945* (Penguin Books reprint edition, New York, 2008).

7 Orwell, George. *What is Fascism?* (Tribune, London, 1944).

8 Professor Dennis Dalton, "Power Over People: Classical and Modern Political Theory, part I," The Teaching Company, 1998, http://www.filedump.net/dumped/ttcpoweroverpeopleclassicalandmodernpoliticaltheory1249137377.pdf

9 Goldman, Emma. *Anarchism: What It Really Stands For* (Mother Earth Publishing Association, 1917).

10 Bray, Mark. *Antifa: The Antifascist Handbook* (Melville House Publishing, New York, 2017) p. 38, 40–4.

11 Bray, Mark. *Antifa: The Antifascist Handbook* (Melville House Publishing, New York, 2017) p. 38, 43–4.

12 Bray, Mark. *Antifa: The Antifascist Handbook* (Melville House Publishing, New York, 2017) p. 38, 43.

13 Jasmine Aguilera, "NYPD Presence Increasing in Jewish Communities After Monsey Stabbing and String of Anti-Semitic Attacks in New York." *Time*, December 30, 2019, www.time.com/5756065/new-york-city-anti-semitic-attacks/.

14 Emily Zanotti, "The Guardian Angels Will Patrol Brooklyn, Jewish Neighborhoods After Spate Of Anti-Semitic Attacks" The Daily Wire, December 29, 2019, www.dailywire.com/news/the-guardian-angels-will-patrol-brooklyn-jewish-neighborhoods-after-spate-of-anti-semitic-attacks.

15 "CAN Mission Statement," Campus Antifascist Network, www.campusantifascistnetwork.com/can-mission-statement/.

16 "Find a Chapter," Young Democratic Socialists of America, August 8, 2020, y.dsausa.org/get-involved/chapters/.

17 George Leef, "UNC Keeps an 'Antifa' Type on its Faculty," *National Review*, July 29, 2019, https://www.nationalreview.com/corner/unc-keeps-an-antifa-type-on-its-faculty/.

18 Anthony Gockowski, "Dartmouth Prof to Donate Half of Book Proceeds to Antifa," *Campus Reform*, November 2017, campusreform.org/?ID=10151.

19 Sean Philip Cotter, "Judge to Anti-Straight Pride Protestors: 'Stay out of Boston,'" *Boston Herald*, September 3, 2019, https://www.bostonherald.com/2019/09/03/stay-out-of-boston-judge-tells-anti-straight-pride-protesters.

20 Valerie Richardson, "'Squad' Democrats Whip up Donations for Activist Arrested in Antifa-Fueled 'Straight Pride' Protest," *The Washington Times*, September 2, 2019, www.washingtontimes.com/news/2019/sep/2/alexandria-ocasio-cortez-ayanna-pressley-push-fund/.

21 Marisa Iati and Hannah Knowles, "ICE Detention-Center Attacker Killed by Police Was an Avowed Anarchist, Authorities Say," *The Washington Post*, July 19, 2019, https://www.washingtonpost.com/nation/2019/07/19/ice-detention-center-attacker-killed-by-police-was-an-avowed-anarchist-authorities-say/.

22 Geneva Sands, "FBI Investigating Shots Fired at ICE Offices in San Antonio," CNN, August 13, 2019, https://www.cnn.com/2019/08/13/politics/fbi-investigating-shots-fired-ice-offices-san-antonio/index.html.

23 Ibid. 7

24 "Germans Slaughter Italian Civilians," History, November 5, 2009, https://www.history.com/this-day-in-history/germans-slaughter-italian-civilians.

25 Foot, John. *Italy's Divided Memory* (Palgrave MacMillan, New York, 2009), https://books.google.com/books?id=DSnFAAAAQBAJ&pg=PA179&lpg=PA179&dq=&source=bl&ots=H7Fmmx5Qe0&sig=Epd3-fuo1O6iIpOR8IadYpfkvW8&hl=fi&sa=X&ved=2ahUKEwir_47DxrTfAhWi_CoKHR29DesQ6AEwBnoECAgQAQ#v=onepage&q&f=false.

26 Pablo Ordaz, "EL GRAPO Mata Para Sobrevivir," El Pais, February 25, 2006, https://elpais.com/diario/2006/02/26/espana/1140908414_850215.html.

27 Robert Beckhusen, "In Manifesto, Mexican Eco-Terrorists Declare War on Nano-technology," *Wired*, March 12, 2013, https://www.wired.com/2013/03/mexican-ecoterrorism/.

28 Bray, Mark. *Antifa: The Antifascist Handbook* (Melville House Publishing, New York, 2017) p. XV.

29 Lois Beckett, "Anti-Fascists Linked to Zero Murderers in the US in 25 Years," *The Guardian*, July 27, 2020, https://www.theguardian.com/world/2020/jul/27/us-rightwing-extremists-attacks-deaths-database-leftwing-antifa?fbclid=IwAR2crupUym2-GmkzuLQKwvFKck1kemN0ErPG-zvTROiS_IcyLsZNngDtvbE.

30 Jessica Kwong, "Who was Bernell Trammell? The Black Trump Supporter Who was Shot Dead Outside His Own Business," *The Sun*, July 27, 2020, https://www.the-sun.com/news/1208492/bernell-trammell-black-trump-supporter-shot-dead/.

31 Bray, Mark. *Antifa: The Antifascist Handbook* (Melville House Publishing, New York, 2017).

32 "San Pedro Anarchist Historical Tour," The Black Rose Society, Los Angeles Indymedia, June 19, 2011. https://la.indymedia.org/calendar/event_display_detail.php?event_id=8747.

33 Bray, Mark. Antifa: The Antifascist Handbook (Melville House Publishing, New York, 2017) p. 203.

34 Bray, Mark. Antifa: The Antifascist Handbook (Melville House Publishing, New York, 2017).

Chapter 4

1 Matt Davis, "What are 'Black Bloc' Anarchists?," Big Think, February 8, 2019, https://bigthink.com/politics-current-affairs/what-are-black-bloc-anarchists?rebelltitem=2#rebelltitem2.

2 Professor Watchlist, "Professor Profile: Eric Clanton," https://professorwatchlist.org/professor/ericclanton.

3 "How 4Chan Doxxing Led to the Arrest of a College Professor," Allee Manning with Jeff Andrews, June 14, 2014, Vocativ, https://www.vocativ.com/news/434611/4chan-doxxing-arrest-eric-clanton/index.html.

4 Emilie Raguso, "Eric Clanton Takes 3-Year Probation Deal in Berkeley Rally Bike Lock Assault Case," August 8, 2018, www.berkeleyside.com/2018/08/08/eric-clanton-takes-3-year-probation-deal-in-berkeley-rally-bike-lock-assault-case.

5 "Propaganda by Deed," Genius Media Group, https://genius.com/A-political-propaganda-by-deed-lyrics.

6 "Leftist Protestors Disrupt Pro-America Speech at UCLA, Police Get Involved," Slightly Offens*ve channel, YouTube, https://www.youtube.com/watch?v=G4-rvm53e9w.

7 Katy Steinmetz, "Fighting Words: A Battle in Berkeley Over Free Speech," Time, June 1, 2017, https://time.com/4800813/battle-berkeley-free-speech/.

8 *National Advancement for the Advancement of Colored People v. Alabama ex rel. Patterson, Attorney General.* 377 U.S. 288, 84 S. Ct. 1302, 12 L. Ed. 2d 325 (1964), https://law.justia.com/.

9 *Chaplinsky v. State of New Hampshire*, 315 U.S. 568, 62 S. Ct. 766, 86 L. Ed. 1031, U.S. 851 (1942)

10 Ibid.

11 Cleve R. Wootson Jr. and Herman Wong, "After Calling Barbara Bush an 'Amazing Racist,' a Professor Taunts Critics: 'I Will Never be Fired," *The Washington Post*, April 19, 2018, https://www.washingtonpost.com/news/grade-point/wp/2018/04/18/after-calling-barbara-bush-an-amazing-racist-a-professor-taunts-critics-i-will-never-be-fired/.

12 *Harry Connick Sr. v. Sheila Myers.* 461 U.S. 138, 103 S. Ct. 1684, 75 L. Ed. 2d 708 (1983).

13 David L. Hudson Jr., "Public Employees, Private Speech: 1st Amendment Doesn't Always Protect Government Workers," *ABA Journal*, May 1, 2017, www.abajournal.com/magazine/article/public_employees_private_speech.

14 Bradley Zint, Alex Chan, Priscella Vega, "OCC Suspends Student Who Recorded Professor's Anti-Trump Comments; Appeal is Filed," *Daily Pilot*, February 15, 2017, https://www.latimes.com/socal/daily-pilot/tn-dpt-me-occ-student-20170215-story. html.

15 "Recall Board if OCC Student Isn't Reinstated," Orange County Register, February 19, 2017, https://www.ocregister.com/2017/02/19/recall-board-if-occ-student-isnt-reinstated/.

16 Matthiesen, Wickert & Lehrer, .S.C., Attorneys at Law, "Laws on Recording Conversations in All 50 States," last updated October 24, 2019, https://www.mwl-law.com/ wp-content/uploads/2018/02/RECORDING-CONVERSATIONS-CHART.pdf.

17 Addison Smith, "Campus Reform Reporter Says Syracuse Professors are Targeting Her," Campus Reform, February 28, 2020, https://www.campusreform.org/?ID=14450.

18 "Racist Professor Recorded Teaching Anti-White Curriculum," Michael Moreno channel, YouTube, October 26. 2019, https://www.youtube.com/watch?v=YjvmI FrX1xQ.

19 "WSU Investigating me for Exposing my Racist Professor," Michael Moreno channel, YouTube, December 11, 2019, https://youtu.be/BV3xSHwUNK8.

20 Mairead McArdle, "Judge Allows Criminal Trial to Proceed Against Pro-Life Investigators," *National Review*, December 6, 2019, https://www.nationalreview.com/news/ judge-allows-criminal-trial-to-proceed-against-pro-life-investigators/.

21 Elias Mooring, "Majority of Audience Stages Walk Out of Spencer's Talk, *The Stanford Daily*, November 15, 2017, https://www.stanforddaily.com/2017/11/15/ reports-of-physical-altercations-surface-following-spencers-visit/.

22 Ali Harrison, "Michael Knowles' Lecture Disrupted by Protestors at UMKC," *The Patriot*, April 17, 2019, https://smsouthnews.com/13428/opinions/michael-knowles -lecture-disrupted-by-protestors-at-umkc/.

23 Rob Picheta, "Man Who Threw ilkshake at Nigel Farage Ordered to Pay Suit-Cleaning Bill," CNN, June 18, 2019, https://www.cnn.com/2019/06/18/uk/nigel-farage-milk-shake-sentence-gbr-intl/index.html.

24 Robby Soave, "Antifa Mob Viciously Assaults Journalist Andy Ngo at Portland Rally," *Reason*, June 29, 2019, https://reason.com/2019/06/29/antifa-andy-ngo-mob -milkshake-violence/.

25 Alan Mastrangelo, "Watch: Leftist mob Harasses College Republicans, Turning Point USA Members at Binghamton U," Breitbart, November 18, 2019, https://www. breitbart.com/tech/2019/11/18/watch-leftist-mob-harasses-college-republicans-turn-ing-point-usa-members-at-binghamton-u/.

26 Adam Sabes, "Video: Two Arrested After 'Antifa' Shuts Down Campus Conservative Event," November 19, 2019, https://www.campusreform.org/?ID=14008.

27 @bingcollegedems, Instagram, November 15, 2019, https://www.instagram.com/p/ B45axQkgJkQ/?utm_source=ig_web_copy_link.

ENDNOTES

28 Dede Ogbueze, "Trump Supporters Met With Opposition by Students Before Freshman Convocation," *Daily Sundial*, September 14, 2017, https://sundial.csun.edu/112468/news/trump-supporters-met-with-opposition-by-students-before-freshman-convocation/.

29 Margherita Beale and Kameron Schmid, "Crowd Gathers Around Sac State Trump Supporters Protesting Stephon Clark Coverage," *The State Hornet*, March 7, 2019, https://statehornet.com/2019/03/crowd-gathers-around-sac-state-trump-supporters-protesting-stephon-clark-coverage/.

30 Hannah Knowles, "A Conservative Gun Rights Activist was Tailed Off campus by a Swarm of Mocking Protestors," *The Washington Post*, February 18, 2020, https://www.washingtonpost.com/education/2020/02/18/gun-girl-kaitlin-ohio-university/.

31 *Clarence Brandenburg v. State of Ohio*. 395 U.S. 444, 89 S. Ct. 1827, 23 L. Ed. 2d 430 (1969).

32 David Aaro, "3 Arrested in Tulane Dorm Room Arson Fire of YAL-member Students," Fox News, March 24, 2019, https://www.foxnews.com/us/police-book-3-in-connection-with-reportedly-targeted-dorm-room-fire.

33 Jon Street, "Incoming Texas Freshmen Threatened with Doxxing if They Join Conservative Campus Groups," Campus Reform, June 21, 2019, https://www.campusreform.org/?ID=13363.

34 Brian Min, "UT Austin Officials Respond to Doxxing Threat Against Conservative Students," The College Fix, July 9, 2019, https://www.thecollegefix.com/ut-austin-officials-respond-to-doxxing-threat-against-conservative-students/.

35 @AsiaJannelll, Twitter, https://twitter.com/AsiaJannelll/status/1266626927885873152.

36 "Protestors Form Human Shield to Protect Police Officer Separated From His Unit," Caldron Pool, May 31, 2020, https://caldronpool.com/protesters-form-human-shield-to-protect-police-officer-separated-from-his-unit/.

37 Anthony Gockowski, "Video: Conservative Activist Attacked by Protestors," Campus Reform, October 12, 2017, https://www.campusreform.org/Video/?ID=9961.

38 Damien Gayle and Ben Quinn, "Extinction Rebellion Rush-Hour Protest Sparks Clash on London Underground," *The Guardian*, October 17, 2019, https://www.theguardian.com/environment/2019/oct/17/extinction-rebellion-activists-london-underground.

39 David Montgomery and Manny Fernandez, "Motorist Who Shot a Protester in Austin Claims Self-Defense," *The New York Times*, July 31, 2020, https://www.nytimes.com/2020/07/31/us/austin-protest-shooting-foster-perry.html.

40 Dave Urbanski, "Surrounding Protesters Start Smashing Up Your Car. You Fear For Your Life. What Can You Legally Do?," *TheBlaze*, September 23, 2017, https://www.theblaze.com/news/2017/09/23/surrounding-protesters-start-smashing-up-your-car-you-fear-for-your-life-what-can-you-legally-do.

Chapter 5

1 Lauren Cooley, "Young Americans for Liberty Sues UC-Berkeley for Refusing to Recognize Them," *Washington Examiner*, December 4, 2017, www.washingtonexaminer.com/young-americans-for-liberty-sues-uc-berkeley-for-refusing-to-recognize-them.

2 Greg Piper, "Worcester State Seems Unaware It's a Public University With First Amendment Obligations," The College Fix, April 23, 2020, https://www.thecollegefix.com/worcester-state-seems-unaware-its-a-public-university-with-first-amendment-obligations/?fbclid=IwAR21l2o9bsM-XVyQgdJ5RGsyAw-HBlvXYx0Oy6HkoPbxBGFzdcQmm-aef9k.

3 Greg Piper, "Pro-Life Students Win Lawsuit Against Public University for Biased Funding Process," The College Fix, August 15, 2019, www.thecollegefix.com/pro-life-students-win-lawsuit-against-public-university-for-biased-funding-process/.

4 "Department of Justice Files Statement of Interest in FIRE Lawsuit," The FIRE, October 25, 2017, www.thefire.org/department-of-justice-files-statement-of-interest-in-fire-lawsuit/.

5 Bradford Richardson, "Liberal Professors Outnumber Conservatives Nearly 12 to 1, Study Finds," *The Washington Times*, October 6, 2016, www.washingtontimes.com/news/2016/oct/6/liberal-professors-outnumber-conservatives-12-1/.

6 Abigail Marone, "Georgetown Prof: White GOP Senators in Kavanaugh Hearing 'Deserve Miserable Deaths,'" Campus Reform, September 30, 2018, https://www.campusreform.org/?ID=11369.

7 Grace Gottschling, "Prof Says Feminists Have 'Every Right' to 'Hate Men,'" Campus Reform, June 11, 2018, https://www.campusreform.org/?ID=11006.

8 Jon Street, "UT-Austin Instructor: Trump 'Is a Nazi' and 'You Are Too If You Still Support Him,'" Campus Reform, August 26, 2019, https://www.campusreform.org/?ID=13603.

9 Celine Ryan, "Berkeley 'Instructor': 'Rural Americans' Are 'Bad People,'" Campus Reform, November 8, 2019, https://www.campusreform.org/?ID=13975.

10 Matthew Adimando, "Sociology prof swears at conservative student during class" Campus Reform, April 17, 2018, https://www.campusreform.org/?ID=10790.

11 Peter Van Voorhis, "Student Suspended for Recording 'Act of Terrorism' Prof," Campus Reform, February 15, 2017, https://www.campusreform.org/?ID=8790.

12 Jon Street, "Professors Worried Students Will Share Lectures With 'Right Wing Sites,'" Campus Reform, March 19, 2020, https://www.campusreform.org/?ID=14563.

13 Jon Street, "Professor Caught Calling Rupert Murdock 'Anti-Immigrant,' Suggests Fox News Founder is Racist," Campus Reform, April 30, 2020, https://www.campusreform.org/?ID=14801.

14 Peter, Van Voorhis, "CSUF Prof Allegedly Assaults Conservative Student on Campus," Campus Reform, February 9, 2017, https://www.campusreform.org/?ID=8763.

15 Corky Siemaszko, "Mizzou Media Professor Melissa Click Charged With Siccing 'Muscle' On Reporter," NBC News, January 25, 2016, https://www.nbcnews.com/news/us-news/mizzou-media-professor-melissa-click-charged-siccing-muscle-reporter-n503871.

16 Stanislav Vysotsky, "Antifa in America: Militant Anti-Fascism Isn't Terrorism, It's Self-defense," Haaretz, March 7 2019, https://www.haaretz.com/world-news/.premium-antifa-in-america-militant-anti-fascism-isn-t-terrorism-it-s-self-defense-1.7425726.

17 "Equinox, Soulcycle Face Boycott Calls. Transcript: 8/8/19, All In w/ Chris Hayes," MSNBC, August 8, 2019, http://www.msnbc.com/transcripts/all-in/2019-08-08.

18 Christian Toto, "Flashback: CNN's Bell Praises Antifa, Curses Tucker Carlson," MRC NewsBusters, July 4, 2019, https://www.newsbusters.org/blogs/nb/christian-toto/2019/07/04/flashback-cnns-bell-praises-antifa-curses-tucker-carlson.

19 Brian Flood, "'This is CNN? Network Apparently Recently Glorified ICE Detention Center Attacker," Fox News, July 15, 2019, https://www.foxnews.com/entertainment/cnn-antifa-ice-glorified.

20 Ibid.

21 Elizabeth Weise, "'How Dare You?' Read Greta Thunberg's Emotional Climate Change Speech to UN and World Leaders," USA Today, September 23, 2019, https://www.usatoday.com/story/news/2019/09/23/greta-thunberg-tells-un-summit-youth-not-forgive-climate-inaction/2421335001/.

22 Charlotte Alter, Suyin Haynes, and Justin Worland, "2019 Person of the Year," Time, www.time.com/person-of-the-year-2019-greta-thunberg/.

23 Adam Sabes, "Video Clown With Bike Horn Shuts Down College Republicans Event," Campus Reform, September 20, 2019. www.campusreform.org/?ID=13734.

24 Nigel Roberts, "Here's What All The Fuss is About Over Rep. Keith Ellison's Antifa Tweet," NewsOne, January 4, 2018, https://newsone.com/3767623/keith-ellison-antifa-tweet-charlottesville-berkeley-donald-trump-book/.

25 Mark Moore, "Minnesota Attorney General Keith Ellison's Son Declares Support for ANTIFA," New York Post, June 1, 2020, https://nypost.com/2020/06/01/minnesota-ag-keith-ellisons-son-declares-support-for-antifa/.

26 Rishika Dugyala, "Ilhan Omar Says Protests Valid, Destruction Not," Politico, May 31, 2020, https://www.politico.com/news/2020/05/31/ilhan-omar-george-floyd-protests-291722.

27 Valerie Richardson, "Ted Wheeler, Portland Mayor, Stands by Decision to Allow Antifa to Block Traffic," Associated Press, October 14, 2018, https://apnews.com/04cf8aabbee571a6c891ad45b1452862.

28 "Ted Wheeler Event Expresses Support for Antifa," Andy Ngo channel, https://www.youtube.com/watch?v=p_YrFPffN1o.

29 Ted Cruz, @tedcruz, Twitter, June 30, 2019https://twitter.com/tedcruz/status/1145212985692119041?.

30 Emily Zanotti, "Portland Protesters Copy Seattle, Form 'Autonomous Zone' and Kick Out Cops," *The Daily Wire*, July 15, 2020, https://www.dailywire.com/news/ portland-protesters-copy-seattle-for-autonomous-zone-and-kick-out-cops.

31 Ibid.

32 Ibid.

33 "Portland Protest: Man Caught on Video Attacking a U.S. Marshal With a Hammer," ABC7 channel, YouTube, July 17, 2020, https://www.youtube.com/ watch?v=t7vlKbR3Gcs.

34 Ryan Saavedra, "Watch: Protesters Burn Bibles in Portland, Rip Protective Boarding Off Buildings," The Daily Wire, August 1, 2020, https://www.dailywire.com/news/ watch-protesters-burn-bibles-in-portland-rip-protective-boarding-off-buildings.

35 Kate Shellnutt, "George Floyd Left a Gospel Legacy in Houston," *Christianity Today*, May 28, 2020, https://www.christianitytoday.com/news/2020/may/george-floyd-min-istry-houston-third-ward-church.html.

36 Pardes Seleh, "CSULA Defends Professor Who Physically Threatened Students for Organizing Shapiro Event," *The Daily Wire*, February 23, 2016, https://www.dailywire. com/news/csula-defends-professor-who-physically-threatened-pardes-seleh.

37 "Challenges to the Freedom of Speech on College Campuses: Part II, Joint Hearing before the Subcommittee on Healthcare, Benefits, and Administrative Rules and the Subcommittee on Intergovernmental Affairs of the Committee on Oversight and Government Reform House of Representatives, One Hundred Fifteenth Congress, second session, serial no. 115-105, May 22, 2018, https://www.govinfo.gov/content/ pkg/CHRG-115hhrg32667/pdf/CHRG-115hhrg32667.pdf.

38 Nikita Vladimirov, "Exclusive: Weinstein's Lengthy Struggle at Evergreen State," Campus Reform, September 7, 2017, https://www.campusreform.org/?ID=9722.

39 Bret Weinstein, "The Campus Mob Came for Me—and You, Professor, Could Be Next," *The Wall Street Journal*, May 30, 2017, https://www.wsj.com/articles/the-campus-mob -came-for-meand-you-professor-could-be-next-1496187482.

40 Ibid.

Chapter 6

1 Douglas E. Streusand, "What Does Jihand Mean?," Middle East Forum, pp. 9–17, September 1997, https://www.meforum.org/357/what-does-jihad-mean.

2 Evan Perez and Jason Hoffman, "Trump Tweets Antifa Will Be Labeled a Terror-ist Organization But Experts Believe That's Unconstitutional," CNN, May 31, 2020, https://www.cnn.com/2020/05/31/politics/trump-antifa-protests/index.html.

3 "Attorney General William P. Barr's Statement on Riots and Domestic Terror-ism," United States Department of Justice, May 31, 2020, justice.gov/opa/pr/ attorney-general-william-p-barrs-statement-riots-and-domestic-terrorism/.

4 "Annual Country Reports on Terrorism," 22 U.S. Code § 2656f.

ENDNOTES

5 "Part II: New Investigation Uncovers Plot to Chain the Trains & Shut down DC During Inauguration," Project Veritas channel, YouTube, January 17, 2017, https://www.youtube.com/watch?v=xIjbkYLI1nY.

6 Ibid. 99

7 Ibid. 131

8 Peter Bergen, "Trump's Crazy Designation of Antifa as Terrorist Organization," CNN, June 1, 2020, https://www.cnn.com/2020/05/31/opinions/trump-antifa-domestic-terrorist-bergen/index.html.

9 Emily Shugerman, "Americas J20 Protests: All You Need to Know About the Nearly 200 People Facing 60 Years in Jail For Protesting Trump," *The Independent,* November 16, 2017, https://www.independent.co.uk/news/world/americas/j20-trump-protests-trials-jail-threat-inauguration-demonstrations-explained-a8057521.html.

10 GianCarlo Canaparo, "Crack Down on Antifa using Law Targeting Organized Crime," The Heritage Foundation, August 6, 2019, https://www.heritage.org/crime-and-justice/commentary/crack-down-antifa-using-law-targeting-organized-crime.

11 California Code, Penal Code—PEN § 186.26, https://codes.findlaw.com/ca/penal-code/pen-sect-186-26.html.

12 Ewan Palmer, "Popularity OF Socialism Spiking in U.S., With 43 Percent Now Saying It Would Be Good for the Country," Newsweek, May 21, 2019, https://www.newsweek.com/socialism-america-gallup-poll-1431266.

13 "New Report Reveals Some 15% of Italians Believe Holocaust Never Happened," i24News, January 31, 2020, https://www.i24news.tv/en/news/international/europe/1580466023-new-report-reveals-some-15-of-italians-believe-holocaust-never-happened.

Chapter 7

1 "United Nations Strategy and Plan of Action on Hate Speech," United Nations, May 2019, https://www.un.org/en/genocideprevention/documents/advising-and-mobilizing/Action_plan_on_hate_speech_EN.pdf.

2 Ibid.

3 "Hate Crimes in the OSCE Region—Incidents and Responses: Annual Report for 2011," Office for Democratic Institutions and Human Rights, November 16, 2012, https://www.osce.org/odihr/102099.

4 Ibid.

5 Ibid.

6 Amendment 12, U.S. Constitution.

7 Peter Hasson, "Bias-Free Language Guide Claims the Word 'American' is 'Problematic,'" Campus Reform, July 28, 2015, https://www.campusreform.org/?ID=6697.

8 Greg Lukianoff and Jonathan Haidt, "The Coddling of the American Mind," *The Atlantic,* September 2015, https://www.theatlantic.com/magazine/archive/2015/09/the-coddling-of-the-american-mind/399356/.

9   Ibid.

10 Alex Morey, "President Obama Echoes FIRE: College Students Shouldn't Be 'Coddled and Protected From Different Points of View' (Transcript)" FIRE, September 15, 2015, https://www.thefire.org/transcript-president-obama-echoes-fire-college-students-shouldnt-be-coddled-and-protected-from-different-points-of-view/.

11 Catherine Shoard, "U.S. Critic: 'Undeniably Racist' Gone with the Wind Should Be Banned from Cinemas," The Guardian, June 25, 2015, https://www.theguardian.com/film/2015/jun/25/us-critic-deniably-racist-gone-with-the-wind-should-be-banned-from-cinemas.

12 "President Obama's Speech To the UN General Assembly – Full Transcript," The Guardian, September 25, 2012, https://www.theguardian.com/world/2012/sep/25/obama-un-general-assembly-transcript.

13 *National Association for the Advancement of Colored People v. Button, Attorney General of Virginia.* 371 U.S. 415, 83 S. Ct, 328, 9 L. Ed. 2d 405 (1963).

14 *The New York Times Company v. L.B. Sullivan.* 376 U.S. 254, 84 S. Ct. 710, 11 L. Ed. 2d 686 (1964).

15 *Hustler Magazine and Larry C. Flynt, Petitioners v. Jerry Falwell.* 485 U.S. 46, 108 S. Ct. 876, 99 L. Ed. 2d 41 (1988).

16 College Pulse, "Free Expression on College Campuses," Knight Foundation, May 2019, https://kf-site-production.s3.amazonaws.com/media_elements/files/000/000/351/original/Knight-CP-Report-FINAL.pdf.

17 Alan Calderon and Helary Yakub, "Request for Action by the ASUCI Senate," legislation number R53-77, February 27, 2018, https://www.asuci.uci.edu/legislative/legislations/print.php?cnum=R53-77&gov_branch=ASUCI\.

18 Laurie Kellman, "House Speaker Pelosi Rebukes Reporter: 'Don't Mess With Me'," *National Catholic Reporter*, December 6, 2019, https://www.ncronline.org/news/politics/house-speaker-pelosi-rebukes-reporter-dont-mess-me.

Chapter 8

1   "Josh Brahm," Equal Rights Institute, https://equalrightsinstitute.com/leadership-team/josh-brahm/.

2   Marty Johnson, "Gowdy Remembers Political Opponent, Good Friend Elijah Cummings," The Hill, October 18, 2019, https://thehill.com/homenews/house/466467-gowdy-remembers-his-political-opponent-and-good-friend-elijah-cummings.

3   Redneck Revolt, https://www.redneckrevolt.org/contact.

4   Ibid. 55

5   Timothy McLaughlin, "The Anger of Hong Kong's Youth," *The Atlantic*, September 22, 2019, https://www.theatlantic.com/international/archive/2019/09/hong-kongs-students-continue-fight/598183/.

6 Jim Powell, "Militant Nonviolence: A Biography of Martin Luther King, Jr.," Libertarianism.org, July 4, 2000, https://www.libertarianism.org/publications/essays/militant-nonviolence-biography-martin-luther-king-jr?fbclid=IwAR0YVdFQpsMgd-1QO8O184y_8BObxLBrOZPpER5UXAYDw2CtK3IrB6sMJsEY.

7 Ibid.

8 Dwane Brown, "How One Man Convinced 200 Ku Klux Klan Members to Give Up Their Robes," NPR, August 20, 2017, npr.org/2017/08/20/544861933/how-one-man-convinced-200-ku-klux-klan-members-to-give-up-their-robes.

PERSONAL ACKNOWLEDGMENTS

To my parents: every day I think of you and the sacrifices you made for my siblings and me. I am lucky to be your son.

To my brother and sister: we lived through the same experiences, and yet we faced our struggles differently. No matter what, we will always have one another.

To Morton: you are an inspiration to all conservatives, especially me.

To my colleagues at the Leadership Institute: thank you for bearing with me while I wrote this and bugged you guys for advice, especially Celtin, Trevor, Ryan, Karla, and Katherine. I could not have written this without your help.

To Adam: without you, I would have never embarked on my conservative journey.

To Kristin and Bryan: thank you for giving me the opportunity to help conservative students.

To all the victims of political violence: you deserved better.

ABOUT THE AUTHOR

Gabriel Nadales is the Leadership Institute's Student Rights Advocate. Originally from Los Angeles, Gabriel has been politically active for over ten years and has spoken at dozens of universities throughout the country to expose the extreme left.

Made in the USA
Columbia, SC
10 November 2020